TRANSITIONS

Copyright by Run With It
All rights reserved
Printed in the United States

No part of this book may be reproduced or transmitted in any form or by any other means, electronic, graphic, optical, or mechanical, including photocopying, recording, taping, filming, electronic data, internet, packets, or by any other information storage or retrieval method without prior written permission of the author.

Transitions
Based on the life of Rose Louise Hammond and written by Rose L. Hammond

1. Transitions – Interviews
2. Transitions – Portraits

Non-fiction publication

ISBN 978-0-692-84508-0
Library of Congress Control Number: 2017907455

Book cover design: Rose L. Hammond
Cover photograph: Rose L. Hammond, Hammond Family
                      Home, Onion Fields

The author gratefully acknowledge permission from Family for use of photos.

For information contact: Run With It, P.O. Box 1419, Grand Rapids, MI 49501-1419 or rdarlene22@hotmail.com

TRANSITIONS

(A coming of age story)

Rose Hammond

Also by Rose Hammond

Non-Fiction Books Based on Individual Life Stories

Gift Book
Idlewild & Woodland Park, MI
(An African American Remembers)

Novel
Just a Poor Country Girl

AUTHOR'S NOTE

The summer of 1986 I returned home with six bags of dirty clothes and a three-year-old who was innocent and had no idea of what brought us back to my home. Drug addiction and depression is a powerful weapon where few are able to let go. I was one of the fortunate ones, but it wasn't an easy decision.

Leaving a husband and all of my accomplishments behind burnt my sole, but I knew the only way for me and my son to survive was to start over where my roots began. I was told by more than one friend that whenever I feel depressed or want to walk the streets again to write. . .just write. At the time I wasn't ready. Now, I'm ready.

The story begins with my youth and ends in the adult years, so that people will have a sense of where I came from and what led up to my demise. Transitions is part of a series.

But, this story couldn't be told without acknowledging a number of people. The Lord above who gave me courage to write the story. Astin Martin, my son, who provided inspiration and courage. Kelly Benton, Steven Jones, Melvin Hammond, Fred Hammond, Larry Hammond, Doneal Hammond, Aunt Lillie, the West Michigan Writers Workshop and above all our Mama, Missionary Charley Louise Hammond Burton.

I decided to use different names for myself, family and cousins because it was easier to write this story from the outside looking in.

Transitions

Part I

Chapter 1

"Where the north begins and the pure waters flow." That's what the sign says when you enter into White Cloud from the south side of town.

I'm not sure what makes the water pure or how our small town claimed the right to say we're the beginning of the north, but this is where we lived.

* * *

During the summer, on the days when we didn't work the fields, Mama loved to eat outside in the front yard.

She'd say, "Maggie, you and Mary get one of those old sheets and spread it across the picnic table."

At once, Mary and I ran towards the house, hollering back, "Okay, Mama."

"Edward and Joe," Mama said, "make sure the table is underneath some shade. And Mike, bring the pot with the hotdogs. Thomas, you can get the mustard, ketchup, and buns. Mary, after you and Maggie spread the tablecloth, grab the paper plates, not the regular plates. I'll get anything else we need."

During dinner time, our family loved to tell stories. Some truthful, some made up.

"Mama," Mike said, "please tell us again how our family found White Cloud. It just seems like a place no one could find."

"Well, kids, it's just like I've told you before. Your grandma met Mrs. Ollie and purchased all of this land that the four houses—Uncle Ted's, Uncle John's, Grandpa Charley's, and ours—are built on."

"All this land," Mike said in a tone of disbelief.

"Yep, all this land," Mama said. She pointed to Uncle Ted's house because it was the closest, "and the rest next to us."

"No," I'd say. "How did we get to White Cloud? You were born down South, right?"

"Yes, I was," Mama said. "But when your grandma left Natchez, Mississippi, she and Aunt Louise, found the family a house in Chicago, Illinois. As I reached my teenage years, she was concerned about the city life and felt the rural area would be best. One day at the bus stop on her way to work, your grandma met a man who convinced her and other coloreds, that's what we were called back then, of a better life in northern Michigan, in a place called Baldwin, Michigan. She checked out his information from other coloreds who had family that followed him up North."

"Really, Mama?" I asked. "No matter how many times you tell us this story, it sounds too good to be true."

"Yes," she said. "The journey wasn't easy. And although he had made this trip many times, on our trip, he made a wrong turn. We drove for what seemed like many miles until we saw a sign for Baldwin, Michigan."

"And what happened next?" Edward asked.

"As I said earlier, your grandma met Mrs. Ollie in

White Cloud at a church gathering, and here we are."

"Who built the houses?" Mike asked.

Mama became quiet. She rubbed the sweat from her forehead. "Your grandma bought all of the land. Uncle Ted, Uncle John, and a couple neighbors helped build the houses."

She became quiet again. "That's when your grandma-" She stared into space. "Your grandma died. She was to move up North after she made more money. On a visit to White Cloud to see our new home, she died. I moved in with Uncle Ted and Aunt Louise because the family didn't want me to live by myself. I was too young to live alone. Only fifteen."

My brothers, sister and I gathered closer to Mama and hugged her. The warm breeze blew the edges of the sheet Mary and I had placed on the picnic table.

Mama said, "Okay, it's your turn, Mike. Pick something around us outside and make up a story. We'll have to look around and see where your story came from."

"Mike's story. That's easy," Thomas said. "It's about the chickens. He always talk about the chickens."

"Nope. Guess again smarty pants. You were chased across the yard screaming for your life and-"

"Aunt Louise," Thomas said.

We laughed.

"Okay, Maggie, your turn."

"Can it be about something that used to be here and can it be a question?"

"I guess so," Mama said.

Mike and Edward looked at me and nodded. They knew exactly what I was about to talk about.

"Daddy. Did the two of you at least love each other?"

Mama didn't answer.

"And before you say it, no, I'm not too young. Other kids who are in the fourth and fifth grade talk about their daddies and mamas who don't live together."

"Your daddy and I were in love. I met him in Chicago on the public transportation. I was going to Madam C. J. Walker School for hair. He was on his way to the factory. He smelled and looked good. He came from a large family. We'd go out, with permission from the family I was living with. See, I lived with a friend and her family while I attended the school."

"Who said hi first?" Mary asked.

"Both of us did. With our eyes. He swept me off my feet."

* * *

Daddy was a tall, dark-skinned, masculine built, and handsome man. He liked to dance and occasionally frequented the bars in Baldwin on the weekends.

On the nights Daddy worked, he'd come home honking the horn as he pulled into the driveway. It wasn't just any honk. It had a beat. Honk. Honk. Pause.

I'd leap from the couch, where I slept, as if one of the springs had coiled forward. I'd run to the back door and hide behind it.

As soon as Daddy turned the door knob and stepped inside the house, I'd surprise him. "Boo!" and hopped onto his leg. Daddy dance walked me to the bedroom where Mama was and gave her a kiss.

My Mama, Charley Louise, named after her Daddy, was shorter than Daddy except when she wore her high heels. She was a petite woman with freckles and light skinned. She didn't visit any of the local bars. The only time I saw her dance was in church when the Holy Ghost took over her body.

One of Mama's favorite pastimes was her flower garden

that lined the driveway.

At times Daddy and Mama seemed very happy except when family members came between them and they argued. It wasn't no secret. Mama's side of the family didn't care for him.

The day was sunny and for once my brothers and I didn't have any bad news to tell Mama from school. When the bus stopped at our driveway Daddy was bent over in his car.

Unaware that we were behind him, Mike startled him. "Hey Daddy."

Daddy turned around bumping his head on the doorway of his car and dropped some clothes.

"What you doin'?" Mike asked.

Daddy looked stunned. "Well, your Mama and I – well, kids I don't know how to tell you this, but I'm moving up the road for a while," he said.

"What!" I said.

"It's nothing that you kids done. But, I'll be just up the road a bit."

"Can we visit you?" Edward asked.

"All the time. I'm sure this is just temporary."

That's how we were told of their separation and Daddy drove out of the driveway.

An hour later when Mama came home, we rushed to her.

"Daddy took his clothes," Mike said.

"Mama, what's happening?" I asked.

"Everything will be alright," she said.

"He left to live up the road," Edward said.

"Yes, for now. But you'll be able to see him."

After Daddy moved out, I sat on the front porch in the over-sized chair writing in my diary.

Up until Daddy left, we all lived in this small house with an outside bathroom. But, he's moved up the road, living in Mrs. Brown's old house who died earlier this year.

I was seven years old when Daddy left. It was a sad day, but we still saw him every day after work. At night when I kneeled to pray for Daddy and Mama to get back together. Week after week, Mama slept with Mary and me.

I continued to write in my diary. *Anyone who says, "Time heals all pain" is a liar. Because us six kids—Mike, fourteen years old, Edward, thirteen, Thomas, nine, twins Joe and Mary, four, and me ten—needed a Daddy. Mama needed her husband. Bills had to be paid.*

* * *

A year later, Mama was hanging clothes on the line. Daddy jostled with Mary and tossed a ball around with the boys. He walked over to Mama. They stood close to each other.

"So, what you told me last week is true. You're leaving?" Mama whispered in Daddy's ear. She didn't know I stood close enough to hear.

Daddy turned around to Mike and Edward. He gave them both hugs. He walked over to Joe, Mary, and Thomas and did the same. My arms were crossed. I leaned against the car.

We all hoped Mama and Daddy would work everything out and he would change his mind. Daddy reached out his arms to me. I slowly reached out to him. I stepped one foot at a time on top of his. We did our last father-daughter dance together. He hugged Mama.

Aunt Louise let her back porch door slam. Daddy turned to her, got in his car, and left. He was gone.

Mama screamed. She yanked the sheets from the clothesline. The clothespins popped off in every direction. I ran behind her, picking them up.

She cried at night and prayed during the day. I don't

know when she stopped crying every night, but her tears lessened and she prayed more. Mary and I continued to share a bed with her.

The weekend Daddy left, I couldn't sleep. I slipped from underneath the covers and slept on the couch, crying.

One thing hadn't changed: the sounds of the rooster. Every morning that cock-a–doodle-doo traveled throughout our house and everyone else's within a three-house radius or more.

The boys' bedroom was in the back of the house, and most times, one of them hollered, "I wish someone would cook that darn thing!"

The day after Daddy left, the house was quiet. Mama wasn't hollering out the chores that she kept taped to the refrigerator door. Pots and pans weren't clattering against the stove from Mike cooking breakfast.

Thomas and I didn't fuss over the TV channels or the bunny ears, trying to get the picture clearer.

Instead, I sat on the top steps in back of the house and listened to the pigs grunt.

Mary sat down next to me. "Maggie, are you all right?"

"Not now, Mary." I watched some of the chickens that had escaped from the coop peck against the ground at the scattered feed sprinkled from last night.

"Mary, I'm sorry." I pulled her close to me. "When Daddy drove away, that hurt all of us."

"It's all right, Maggie. I know you didn't mean to ignore me."

Uncle Ted walked to the wood shop behind his house and looked towards us. "Good morning girls," he said.

"Excuse me, Maggie and Mary," Mike said. "We have chores to do. The animals are probably hungry."

Edward walked to the chickens, but Mike turned around. "You two all right?"

"Should we be?" I responded and called for Tuffy, so that Mary and I could feed him.

The mood was solemn between the four of us. Normally we'd finish our chores quicker so that we could walk up the road and visit daddy. That wasn't necessary, now.

"Maggie," Mama called.

"Over here." Mary and I met Mama in the house.

She gave us a big hug, longer than normal, and whispered in our ear, "Everything will be all right. After you feed Tuffy, could the two of you set the breakfast table?"

Mama sat at one end of the table, and Mike at the other where Daddy used to sit. "I know you guys are wondering what's going happen." Mama looked at each one of us. "This is still a family and I believe that God will see us through any troubled times. Okay?"

"Yes, ma'am," Mike said.

We repeated what Mike had said and finished our breakfast.

* * *

Once School was out, White Cloud didn't have much to offer except for small town fun which our family and neighbors were good at.

Today, in the middle of the week the Harris boys knocked on our front door.

"Come on in," Mike said.

"Edward and Thomas around?"

"Yeah. What's up?"

"Do you guys wanna do something like walk down to the creek?"

"I don't know. It's near our supper time. Maybe we can sneak out for a while, but we'll have to stay close to home. Thomas! Edward!" Mike hollered.

Edward ran out from the bedroom. "What you hollering for? We're right here."

Thomas walked out of the room. "I vote for basketball."

"You guys didn't hear any choices," Mike said.

"I don't care. I vote for basketball," Thomas said.

I sat in the chair in the living room listening to these boys fuss over what to do like they're going to win some money or something.

"Okay, everyone raise your hands if you wanna go down to the creek," Jason Harris said.

Two people raised their hands.

"Now who want to play basketball?" Thomas asked.

One person raised their hand, Thomas.

"Who want to play baseball?" Mike asked.

Two people raised their hands. Slowly Tom Harris changed his mind and raised his.

"That makes three for baseball," Mike said.

"Baseball it is," Mike said. "As long as Mama lets us."

Mama was fixing supper. Usually, my brothers and I helped, but to my surprise, she let them go.

"When I call you, come back home for supper."

The boys were walking out of the house when Mike said. "Is it all right if our sister comes along and plays?"

I got up from the chair before they answered and I walked with haste out the door for fear that if Mama saw me, she might ask me to help with supper.

"Why does she have to come?" Jason asked.

"She's one of the best runners we got and can steal bases," Mike said.

The only game I didn't play with the boys was basketball. Uncle Ted had this pole he secured inside the ground behind the chicken coop.

He had cut a hole in one of the old wooden crates and

nailed it to the pole. It was in an area where there wasn't much grass. Uncle Ted thought the ball would bounce better that way.

It took a short time for Tom, the oldest Harris brother to convince Jason. "Okay, she can play."

While we picked our teams Tom said, "Just a minute. I want to change the game."

"What's that?" Mike asked.

Oh, oh, I thought. Here it comes.

"We'll play four games," Tom said. "After the second game, we can switch players. You can take one of our best players and we'll take one of yours."

Mike, Edward, Thomas, and I huddled up to discuss this for a minute then said, "Agreed."

After playing two games, each side chose one of the other team's players.

"We choose Jason," Mike said.

The Harris' were quiet. Tom said, "We'll choose Maggie."

Jason and I passed each other. He watched me and I watched him as we walked to our new teams.

The first game was won by my brothers with Jason hitting a home run. During the second game, the score was much closer. At first, my brothers' team was winning. My new team, the Harris', rallied back. I was at bat and stole second and third base. The oldest Harris brother was at bat. He swung twice and had two strikes called against him.

Mike was on the pitcher's mound, his arm in the air. I leaned off third base with one foot on.

"Maggie!"

We all looked at our house. Mama leaned out of the screen door, hollering my name for all the world to hear.

"Ma'am," I yelled back.

"I need your help in the house."

Before I left, both teams argued that since I had to leave the game, their team won.

"Maggie, please stop running through the house!" Mama said. "Your sister and brother are napping."

She pointed at the cupboard. "Could you open a jar of canned collard greens and pour them into that pot to cook while the chicken is frying?"

There was scent of the peach cobbler baking in the oven.

"Mama, why do you always call me into the house when I'm playing with the boys?"

"One day, you will be married and will have to cook for your husband."

"What if I don't want to get married?"

"Well, you'll still need to know how to cook. You're going to eat, aren't you?"

I shrugged my shoulders and poured the collard greens from the Ball jar.

The boys stomped into the house, arguing about who had won the game. As usual, Edward argued the loudest.

"Just in time," Mama said in her high-pitched voice that signaled she was in command. "Boys, wash your hands. Mike, you can mix the cornbread and put it in that skillet over there?"

"How do you want me to cook it?" Mike asked. "Like pancakes, or pour all of it into the frying pan at once?"

"What do you kids want?" Mama asked.

"Pancake."

Mama stopped Edward before he went into his bedroom. "Edward, the Kool-Aid is calling your name. Can't you hear it?"

No matter the good or bad times, she figured out a way to make us laugh.

I helped Mama set the dinner plates on the table. When

Edward walked past, I took the opportunity to tease. "Oh, did someone lose?" I asked.

"Maggie, you can turn the fire off from underneath the collard greens," Mama said.

"Mama, the cornbread is ready," Mike said.

"We can put the food on the table," Mama said. "Maggie, I believe it's your turn to say the grace."

"Thank you, God, for the food we are about to eat." I looked around the table and at Mama last and smiled. "And thank you, God, for the collard greens we grew in our backyard with our own hands. Amen."

"That was beautiful, Maggie," Mama said. "I'm quite sure that God loved the reference to the collard greens."

"My grace will be better," Thomas said.

It seemed like everything was a competition in our house. Mama hated that and let us know in her own subtle way.

"That's good, Thomas," she said. "Since you are so enthusiastic, you can bless the food next time. Now, could someone pass the collard greens that we grew with our own hands?"

Thomas ate the fastest. The food was off his plate before anyone else. I don't think he believed in the concept of chewing.

"Slow down," Mama said. "You kids act like this is going to be your last day to eat. Where do you put all of that food? And, so fast?" Mama asked. "You're no bigger than nothing."

Thomas was also the one who'd leave one sip of the Kool-Aid and place the pitcher back inside the refrigerator, just so he wouldn't be blamed for drinking it all.

Mama spread some butter on her cornbread and asked if there was anything that the family had to discuss.

The room became silent. We looked at each other.

"Since no one else has anything to say, I'd like to announce that on Saturday, we will eat at Aunt Louise's house. Everyone has to bring a dish."

Dinner at Aunt Louise's house wasn't unusual. Sometimes it was on Saturdays or after church on Sunday. This was our family's bonding time, a tradition started in Natchez, Mississippi.

"Mama, will you make a cake?" I asked. "Everyone likes your cakes."

"What flavor?"

"Um..."

"Yellow," Edward blurted

"Yeah," I agreed. "Yellow cake."

"Okay, that's what I'll bring. If that's all, let's clean the dinner table."

Chairs scuffled against the wooden floor. Everyone was responsible for taking their own plates into the kitchen. Tonight, Mama and I put the extra food away. She packed it into bowls and wrapped foil around it.

Later, Mary and I were in our bedroom. She played with her dolls, and I wrote in my journal. Mama played a song on the piano, probably one that the church choir was going to sing.

The back door opened and closed. A loud voice said, "Smells like I'm just in time."

It was Aunt Louise. Our families never knocked. We walked in, talking as if we lived with each other. Aunt Louise's voice had an annoying high-pitched sound, like the Wicked Witch.

She was a strong disciplinarian. There were times I wondered if she knew how to be soft or gentle. She must have because Uncle Ted married her, and gentle is exactly how I'd describe him.

"Hi, Aunt Louise," I said, coming out of the bedroom.

"You startled me," Aunt Louise said.

"Sorry," I said. "I didn't mean to."

I'm sure that sometimes Uncle Ted made Aunt Louise smile, but she frowned as she stood by the piano.

"Hey, Charley Louise," she said. "Remember those papers we talked about?"

Mama nodded.

"Well, here they are. Do you want me to look over them with you?"

The boys fussed back and forth in their bedroom.

"Y'all stop whatever it is you're doing to each other," Mama yelled.

"Edward hit me first," Thomas yelled.

"Both of you stop it," Mama said.

Thomas ran out of the bedroom. He and Edward continued to argue.

I hopped on the couch and leaned over the opening in the wall between the kitchen and living room. Mama and Aunt Louise separated the two boys.

"Didn't I tell you kids to stop it?" Mama said with a stern face.

Edward had to sit at the dining room table and Thomas in the living room until Mama decided that the two of them had calmed down enough.

"Maggie, you can go into the bedroom with Mary."

Mama and Aunt Louise continued to talk about the papers. I heard Aunt Louise, but I didn't know what the papers were about.

"You know that Ted, John, Pearl, and I are here to help," Aunt Louise said. "That's what families do, and that's why your mama bought all of this land, so that we could live next to one another."

Mama was an only child. She was in ninth grade when her mama died. Ever since then, Aunt Louise, being one of only two blood relatives, directed Mama's life. Uncle John was the other relative. Mama's father didn't come back into her life until she graduated from high school. Aunt Louise took the place of her mama, which I think caused friction between Mama and Daddy. There were times when both Aunt Louise and Uncle John disciplined us kids. I think because they were grandma's mother and brother, they earned that right.

I went to the kitchen to get a glass of water, pausing to look out the window. Uncle John and Aunt Pearl lived to the right of our house. A small gathering of trees separated our houses. Uncle John had planted a patch of corn on the other side of the trees that also made it hard to see their house. Uncle Ted and Aunt Louise lived to the left of our house.

"Edward, go and sit in the living room with your brother, but in the chair," Mama said. She and Aunt Louise moved into the dining room and sat at the kitchen table.

"With me left to raise these kids, I have bills. School will begin soon, and winter's just a few months away from that. I'm not sure where I'll get help," Mama said.

They must have forgotten for a minute that I was in the kitchen.

"Maggie," Mama said. "I thought I told you to go in the bedroom."

I went to the bedroom but leaned out the door to listen.

"These papers will help you," Aunt Louise said. "You can fill them out to get on welfare. Like I said, Ted and the rest of the family don't mind helping, but you need to help yourself, too."

Before Daddy left, Mama didn't have to do much work other than cleaning the large summer houses near the lake with my aunts.

Other than working part-time at the Fremont Nursing Home, Aunt Louise had Uncle Ted who worked at the Newaygo County Court House in White Cloud. Aunt Pearl had Uncle John who worked at the factory just east of town. Mama, she didn't have that security anymore.

With Daddy gone, the house felt empty. I missed his deep hearty laugh, when he would lift me on his foot as he walked, and when we played baseball across the road in the weeds or basketball on the dirt behind the chicken coop. But what I missed most was having a complete family like other kids with a daddy and mama in the same house.

"Come on," Aunt Louise said to Mama. "Signing up for welfare will help your family."

Mama looked at the papers in her hands and took a deep breath. "But Aunt Louise...I don't know anything about being on welfare."

"Well, I have to go," Aunt Louise said. "Ted is probably waiting for me to set the dinner table. Just think about it. We can discuss this further after dinner tomorrow."

Mama walked Aunt Louise to the door. Then she sat back down at the dining room table, thumbing through the welfare papers with one hand and rubbing her forehead with the other.

I felt her sadness and wondered how we would have money for food and clothes.

Chapter 2

It's Saturday at five o'clock, and time for our family to meet at Uncle Ted and Aunt Louise's house for dinner.

"Boys, go out to the back porch," Uncle Ted said. "There are folded tables behind the couch. Bring two of them."

And as usual, Mike, Edward, Thomas and Joe made this out to be who will beat who to bring the tables inside.

Thomas and Joe carried one together and was ahead of Mike and Edward until Joe stumbled.

Mama turned. "Do you boys have to make a race out of everything?"

In the meantime, Uncle John and Uncle Ted grabbed the leaf to extend the dinner table.

A leaf is an addition to the table, but not always used. You attach it to the center of the table and it pops in. The table is now longer.

The smell of food filled every room. Aunt Pearl brought macaroni and cheese with double cheese and diced ham. Mama brought cakes, string beans, canned from our garden, and fried chicken. Aunt Louise made potato salad, fried corn, and cornbread. Granddaddy brought baked yams and collard greens earlier.

The kids were responsible for the Kool-Aid. Since we couldn't decide between strawberry or grape, we brought both flavors.

My sister and I set the table and folded the napkins.

"Oh, shoot," I said. "Where does this doggone salad fork and soup spoon go?"

Mama came up behind me. She held my hand with the fork and helped me place it. She did the same with the soup spoon.

Aunt Pearl and Aunt Louise began to put the food on the table. The main table had a place reserved in the middle that we called "center stage." Sometimes, it was ham or a big garden salad, greens that we grew in the family garden, rolls that Aunt Pearl baked, or turkey. Today, it was the bowl of fried chicken. I felt sorry for the chickens we had raised, knowing they'd get eaten.

Aunt Louise summoned everyone to the table. "Dinner's ready!"

The seating order was important to Aunt Louise. Uncle Ted and Uncle John sat at the end of the table, their wives and Mama on the sides. Older kids sat at one table, younger kids at the other.

At first, there wasn't much talking or noise except for the spoons that clacked against the bowls and plates. When Daddy was here, he didn't come to many of these Saturday meals, but he was in White Cloud up the road from our houses.

Now with him in Chicago, there was a sense of awkwardness. You could tell that someone wanted to talk about his absence. When we began to tease each other and our voices began to overtake the kitchen, Aunt Louise gave us the evil eye. "You kids be quiet over there," she said.

"No," Mama said softly. "Let them laugh." Mama leaned over from the grownups' table. She smiled at us.

We continued to tease and laugh. Soon the entire room was filled with laughter.

Then Aunt Louise had to bring up the papers.

"Charley Louise, have you had a chance to look over the welfare papers?"

Mama's face turned red. She had a lot of pride and didn't want everyone to know that our family was poor.

"No...not yet," Mama said quietly. Her voice didn't sound convincing.

"I wanted to tell you this sooner," Aunt Louise said, "but wasn't sure until I saw the doctor."

Aunt Louise never got sick. I wondered how this involved Mama.

"Charley Louise," Aunt Louise's voice was soft. "I'll be having surgery. Maybe the facility will let you work in my place until I come back. I'll ask the supervisor."

"Will everything be all right?" Mama asked.

"Your Aunt Louise will be fine," Uncle Ted said. "It's a minor surgery."

The kids' table had become quiet upon hearing the news. Aunt Louise looked over the top of her glasses, her eyebrows lifted, and gave us the longest stare I've ever seen. Mike held the Kool-Aid pitcher in the air as if he didn't dare move.

"Don't worry," she said. "I'll still be able to watch you kids through the dining room window."

I thought, God, we're all sad about Aunt Louise's surgery, but why dampen our dreams?

The window, as the kids called it, was where Aunt Louise sat in her big chair and monitored our every move while we were outside. If we threw dirt, she told Mama. If we argued with each other and it seemed like there was a fight, she told Mama. She probably meant well. But sometimes it seemed like she was the baby-sitter from hell.

The only places where she couldn't see us from the window were behind the big oak tree, garage, and chicken coop. That's where my brothers played basketball with the neighbor kids. I'd run through the rows of collard greens, corn, cucumbers, and tomatoes, chasing butterflies.

Uncle Ted touched Mama's hand. "Charley Louise," he said, "these are rough times for you and the kids, but family takes care of each other."

"Yes," Aunt Pearl said. "So hold your head up. Don't be ashamed."

Mama looked at Mike, Edward, Thomas, Joe, Mary, and me. A smile crept across her face. It seemed like she found strength from us.

She lifted her chin, picked up a forkful of string beans, and smiled bigger.

"I'll look at the papers again after supper," Mama said. "And yes, Aunt Louise, please check on that job."

"First thing," she said.

After everyone had eaten, Mama sensed my reluctance to cleanup. I dodged her attempts to make eye contact. She caught me before I sneaked into the bathroom.

"Maggie, you can help Aunt Pearl. While she clear the dishes from the table, you can put the food away."

"Shoot," I said.

"That's what you get for sneaking away." Edward snickered.

Aunt Louise retired to the living room, sat in her chair in front of the window, and rested.

"Honey, are you going to work on Monday?" Uncle Ted

asked her.

I had scraped the mashed potatoes into a bowl and walked over to the trash, throwing some chicken bones away.

"Stop being so nosey," Aunt Pearl said.

Edward whispered in my ear, "If Uncle Ted wants your advice, he'll ask you, Miss Nosey." He chuckled as he continued to sweep food crumbs.

"Shut up, Edward," I said, wrinkling my forehead.

Thomas expressed his dissatisfaction for having to wash the dishes by splashing a little water on the floor each time he rinsed a plate or cup or pot.

"Stop splashing that water, Thomas," I told him.

"I hate doin' dishes."

Mike laughed. "Boy, you hate doin' any work."

"Hurry up, kids," Mama said. "I want to call Mrs. Harris before it gets too late."

Mrs. Harris lived up the road. She and her four kids received welfare, so I figured Mama wanted to ask her questions. But, I didn't want to be on Welfare having to stand in line for our food.

When the kitchen was cleaned and food put away, my brothers and I raced out of Aunt Louise's house. The screen door slammed behind us.

"Didn't I tell you kids not to slam my screen door?" Aunt Louise yelled.

"Guess she's not too sick," I told my brothers.

Edward and Thomas ran to our house. They grabbed the handle to the back door at the same time causing them to bump into each other.

Mama walked up from behind and caught the two of them wrestling. She tapped Edward and Thomas on their heads. "Why do you boys always have to fight?" Mama asked. "Get in the house."

I turned on the TV to The Ed Sullivan Show all the while listening to Mama continue to fuss at Edward and Thomas.

We had one black and white TV that had three channels. Sometimes Mama let us draw straws to decide who would control the channel for an hour.

Tonight wasn't one of those nights, but since I beat my brothers inside the house, I chose the first show.

Edward hated Ed Sullivan and stomped out of the living room to his bedroom. He'd rather watch a western.

"Joe and Mary," Mama said, "you two sit right here next to Maggie and watch whatever she has on that television set."

Mama picked up the telephone. "Ms. Harris, this is Charley Louise...me and the kids are doing fine." She pulled the telephone cord into the bedroom. She closed the curtain that served as the bedroom door.

I heard the bed springs in her room squeak. Mama spoke softly. With the singing on the television show and Mary and Joe trying to sing along, it was hard to hear.

"Shhh," I told them, but they sung louder.

A half hour later, Mama came out of the bedroom and sat in her favorite chair. It was a puke yellow, flowery chair with an overstuffed seat cushion. She had crocheted doilies on the arm rests of the chair because they were worn down to the wood. Each time the stuffing came out, Mama would stuff it back in.

"Who's on tonight?"

"Some ventriloquist," I said.

* * *

Today seemed hotter than yesterday, but not too hot for Mama.

She kneeled in her flower garden, weeding. I was outside jumping rope with Mary when I heard my name. "Maggie!"

"Yeah Ma!"

"Come help me pull weeds from the flowers."

"Okay. Be right there." I couldn't grunt enough. Mama loved her flowers. But me, let's just say it wasn't my favorite thing to do.

The garden was shaped in a capital L around the driveway with yellow, pink, red, purple and another flower that looked like a weed, but wasn't.

Mama loved her garden. I believed her flowers helped to take her thoughts away from Daddy and her problems. She'd hum or sing to the flowers and had a smile on her face.

She'd tell me a story about each flower when I helped her weed.

One of her favorite flowers was the tulip, and another that looked like the weed. But when I went to pull it she immediately hollered.

"No," she said. "Don't pull those."

"Sorry" was all I could say, not wanting Mama to know I was daydreaming.

"Well, this is all for today. We can pick back up where we stopped tomorrow."

"Hallelujah," I whispered.

"I have to go to town. Go tell Mike I'll be back. He's in charge."

I pretended to walk inside the house until Mama drove out of the driveway. Then Tuffy, our dog, and I chased each other for at least a half hour. I loved to run, and so did he, barking until one of us got tired. Usually, it was me.

I stopped, gasping for air, when Aunt Louise drove into the driveway.

"Where's Mama?" Mike asked me.

"She went to town and said you're in charge."

"Why didn't you come and tell me? And what is Tuffy barking about?"

"I was just about to come inside, but Aunt Louise honked."

Mike looked down at me, knowing I was lying, but Aunt Louise saved the day and called to me.

"When will your mama be back?" she asked.

"Not sure. She went into town," I said.

"When she gets back, tell her to come and see me," Aunt Louise said.

An hour later, Mama came in the house. "You kids put the groceries away. Mike, you handle the hardware stuff."

I waited with anticipation, hardly able to control my curiosity to hear what Aunt Louise wanted to talk to Mama about.

Whatever it was didn't take long before Mama walked back in the house, letting the door slam behind her. "Get your brothers."

"Mike. Thomas," I yelled. "Come inside. Mama wants to talk to us."

Mama told us to sit around the dining room table. She smiled. "I got a job. It's not full time, but it's a start."

We sat at the table, quiet, in shock. Then within seconds, we all clapped and yelled with excitement.

"Wait a minute," I said. "Who's gonna baby-sit?"

Chapter 3

"You kids know Mrs. Ollie, who lives up the road? Well, I spoke with her and she agreed to baby-sit you kids while I'm at work. Mike will oversee that you do your chores."

I knew the twins wouldn't mind having Mrs. Ollie watch them sometimes. She was fun to be around. She was short and very dark complected with a round face, and, just like Aunt Pearl, she had a gold front tooth.

She and her husband lived in a white, one-bedroom home. The house sat on top of a hill and had a creek that ran beside it with quicksand. The creek was called Coldcreek.

During the summer months, even when Mrs. Ollie wasn't baby-sitting, we'd play around the creek.

Mrs. Ollie would yell out her back door many times, "You kids better watch out for quicksand and snakes!"

Most times, Mike, Thomas, Joe, Mary, and me listened, but lingered until she said, "snakes." Edward was stubborn and didn't listen. It was as though he was daring a snake to come after him or the quicksand to grab ahold of his leg.

Mrs. Ollie had the best trees, the branches scattered in just the right directions. There was one with sturdier branches than the others. That's the one I preferred because it was farthest from the creek. And, if I slid off of the branch, there was no quicksand.

When Mrs. Ollie peeked out of her kitchen window and saw that I was near the top of the tree, she'd yell, "Get down from there before you fall and hurt yourself and end up at the hospital."

My brothers, especially Edward, liked to follow the creek, seeing who could hop to the furthest rock without falling into the quicksand. They were daredevils.

Edward liked a challenge and hated when Mike beat him. He looked at Mike with a silly smirk on his face and swung his arms back and forth.

"Don't do it," I said.

Edward acted like he didn't hear me. He bent his knees and jumped, missing the rock, one foot stuck in the quicksand.

"Stop wiggling," Mike hollered. "This quicksand isn't deep enough to swallow anyone."

Mike's voice became more anxious. "Go and get help!"

"Mrs. Ollie!" I ran to the house. "Mrs. Ollie!"

She ran out her back door like there was a fire.

"What's wrong?" she asked. "Is someone hurt?"

"Edward's stuck in your quicksand."

Mrs. Ollie's eyes grew larger than her door knobs. She stumbled down the small incline to the creek. "What did I tell you kids about going back here? Edward, don't move. Thomas, run and get some help," Mrs. Ollie said.

Uncle Ted drove into the driveway. Thomas running behind his truck.

"Ted, help this boy," Mrs. Ollie said.

As he hurried from his truck, Uncle Ted explained,

"Thomas was running out of your driveway just as I was driving by. He flagged me down hollering that Edward was stuck in your quicksand."

"Could you please hurry before the boy pisses in his pants, if he hasn't already?" Mrs. Ollie said.

Uncle John was in the truck with Uncle Ted. They threw Edward a rope. Mrs. Ollie's neighbor came running across his back yard when he saw all of the commotion.

I couldn't believe how scared Edward looked. He was the one who always boasted about how brave he was.

Mrs. Ollie wrapped a towel around him and scolded him at the same time. She swatted his butt. "I told you, didn't I?"

Edward tried to get away from her swats, but she had a strong grip on his arms.

Edward, Mike, and Thomas climbed into the back of Uncle Ted's pickup truck. The twins and I sat in the front. Uncle John stayed to talk with Mrs. Ollie's neighbor.

When we reached our driveway, Uncle Ted parked by his back door. "You'd better clean yourself up before your mama gets home."

On the outside of our house was a hose. Mike sprayed Edward from head to toe underneath the oak tree in our backyard. Tuffy watched as if it was a movie. I sat next to him.

Edward shivered, his hands over his private parts. I think he was still startled.

It was a half hour before Aunt Louise and Mama got back from town.

When they drove into the driveway, Mary and I were playing hopscotch in the back yard. Mike and Thomas were behind the chicken coop playing basketball. Joe was with them. Edward hadn't come out from the house, yet after changing his clothes.

Aunt Louise waved bye to Mama and called for Uncle Ted to help with the groceries.

By the time Uncle Ted came outside to help, Mama was almost at our house. He gave Aunt Louise a kiss and called out to Mama. "Charley Louise," he said with one hand on the roof of their car, "you need to speak to Edward."

"Something happen?" Mama asked.

"Just speak to him."

I felt sorry for Mama. She had to play the role of both a mama and daddy.

"Maggie, get your brothers. We have some groceries to get out of their car," Mama said.

"Mike! Thomas! Joe!" I hollered. "Come help with the groceries." I ran into the house for Edward.

Mama had stopped at her car for something. Edward and I passed her, but she didn't say anything to him. I don't know which was worse. Her not saying anything or the look from her eyes.

Edward carried one bag and went into his bedroom, leaving us to carry the rest.

"Where's Edward?" Mama asked me noticing that he hadn't come back out.

"He went inside his bedroom," I said.

"Are there anymore bags, Mike?" Mama asked.

"No. This is the last one," Mike replied.

Mama slammed our car door and walked inside the house. I wasn't going to miss this for nothing and followed behind her.

"Edward," she called.

He didn't come out from the bedroom fast enough.

"Edward!" Mama called a little louder. "Don't let me have to come in there and get you."

He brushed the curtain back from his bedroom so

hastily that it swung back and forth.

While we took the groceries out, Mama began to fold the grocery bags laying them on top of each other.

"Is there anything special that happened today while I was gone?" Mama asked.

No one dared to answer.

Mama gave us the look—that look that mamas give when they know the secret you think they don't know.

The phone rang. All Mama said was "hello. I'm talking to them all now," and hung up.

I thought, Uh-oh. Uncle Ted must have told her.

"Today at Mrs. Ollie's house..." Edward blurted out.

Mama looked at me and then Mike.

"Today at Mrs. Ollie's house, I was running around with Mike and Thomas. While in her back yard, you know along the creek..." Edward paused for moment. "Well, my foot came from underneath me and I slid into the quicksand, but just the edge. I was able to stop and grab onto a small branch until Uncle Ted came and helped."

Mama was silent. She looked at me and then Mike.

I'm thinking, that story doesn't sound good to me. Mama couldn't believe it.

"Were you two there as well?"

"Yes, ma'am," we answered simultaneously, and immediately added, "but we didn't play around the quicksand."

From the look in Edwards' face, he probably was praying inside that she believed him.

"How many times has Mrs. Ollie told you kids not to run along the creek behind her house?"

"Many times," Mike answered.

Mama plopped into the dining room chair. She twiddled her thumbs, thinking. She stood up, walked into the kitchen, and removed the list of chores from the refrigerator. Then she sat back down and began to erase the chores. She tapped the table with the eraser end of the pencil.

"You scared everyone out of their wits, Edward," Mama said. "And thank God you stumbled where you did."

She looked back down at the list and began writing.

"You should thank your brothers and sisters for being there to help."

Edward turned around. "Thank you, guys, for helpin' me."

"I want you to thank your Uncle Ted and beg Mrs. Ollie's pardon." Mama wiggled her finger at Edward and added, "If Uncle Ted, Uncle John and the neighbor hadn't helped, you'd probably still be wondering how to get out."

Sweat rolled down Edward's forehead.

Typically, we tease each other for getting into trouble. But this time I felt sorry for Edward. He looked scared having to answer to Mama.

"Lastly," Mama said, "I will add a few more chores to your list, but Uncle Ted and Mrs. Ollie can choose what chores. On Saturday, you will go to Mrs. Ollie, her neighbor, Uncle Ted and Uncle John to ask what help they need. I'll talk to them beforehand. I'm headed over to Aunt Louise's. Is there anything else I need to know?"

We answered together, "No, ma'am."

Before she left, Mama taped the new list of chores on the refrigerator. Once she closed the door, Edward was the first to scroll his fingers down the list. We crowded behind him.

After reading the list, the twins and I watched television. The boys sat around the dining room table and played checkers.

I began to grow tired of the television and sat on the front porch to write in my journal. Today I wrote about the quicksand incident and chores.

It wasn't too much later, there were sounds of chairs scooting against the wood floor and Mike's voice in the living room.

"Do you know where Maggie went?" Mike asked the twins.

He came out to the front porch staring out the window up and down the road.

"Mama's been gone a long time," he said.

I didn't respond and kept writing in my journal.

"What do you think of the chores Mama assigned Edward?" Mike asked.

"All I'm concerned about is I'll have help with mine," I said.

"Well, I'm gonna call the Harris' to see if anyone wants to play hide-and-seek," Mike said. "Do you wanna to play?"

"Heck yeah," I answered. "Wait. Are we playin' the regular game or the made up version?"

"Let's ask everyone else before the two of us make that decision," Mike said.

He called the Harris'. Within a short time, we met in our backyard.

"Before we begin, we all have to decide which hide-and-seek to play. The regular or the made up one," Mike said.

"Raise your hand if you want to play the regular game," Mike said. "And the made up one?"

The vote was in with the majority wanting to play the made up game.

"I'll start. Once I count to ten you have to hide," Mike said. "Remember, if I find your hiding place, but you can beat me back to the tree where I stood to count from, you have won and I'll look for the next person. But, if I get back to the tree before you, you have lost and you have to find the next person with me."

Mike stepped onto a twig, so I knew he was close to me. As I thought he was coming from one direction, I moved the other way. He came around the corner and saw me. I ran fast to the tree, almost caught, but I touched the tree first.

Jason and Tom Harris' mama walked up the road and hollered their names one by one. "It's time to come home," she said.

The Harris' were upset with their mama for helping them to lose stomping their feet.

Mama walked from Aunt Louise' house. "Dorsey kids," she said loudly, "you can follow me into our house."

Before we all sat down, Mama asked Mike to get the ice cream from the freezer and for me to get the bowls and spoons.

She made the best homemade ice cream, usually vanilla. She didn't have to worry about turning the handle. She had us six kids to help.

After we ate the ice cream, she talked about a change in our family life.

"Aunt Louise told me that her surgery has been moved up. I'll start work sooner than expected. I met with Mrs. Ollie and she agreed to baby-sit when needed. I'll start Monday, working the day shift part-time."

"Do we know what's wrong with Aunt Louise?" I asked.

"Well, there's something wrong with her stomach and she'll need to have it fixed."

"Will Mrs. Ollie watch us all day long?" Mike asked.

"On the days I'm working, Mrs. Ollie will watch you until Aunt Pearl gets off work just in case I can pick up more hours. Although Aunt Louise can sit in her chair and watch from the window, she will be healing," Mama said.

"What about the chores," Maggie asked.

"Mike will oversee that everyone does their chores. And if I can pick up more hours, Mike, I'd like you to watch the kids until I get home from work. To give Mrs. Ollie and Aunt Pearl a break."

This was the beginning of Mike, the oldest, taking the watchful eye of Daddy's role since he had moved to Chicago. When Mama first started working, the younger kids wouldn't listen to anything Mike said.

If someone was misbehaving outside and it was within Aunt Louise' view, she'd knock on her dining room window, except when we played basketball behind the chicken coop. If we began to fight across the road, she'd sit on their front porch and when Mama came home, she'd report everything.

The Harris boys always said, "I thought she was sick?"

It wasn't until about five weeks after Mama started working that Aunt Pearl came over to our house on Mama's day off.

I was sitting on my bed reading. Aunt Pearl and Mama talked about Aunt Louise, how she was healing and would be back to work soon.

I didn't hear Mama say anything. I sat my book down and leaned in the direction of the bedroom doorway. The curtain wasn't pushed aside. Mama and Aunt Pearl couldn't see that I was listening.

"This part-time job at the facility isn't paying enough for me to feed six kids," Mama said. "Four of them will need school clothes soon, and I'll have to pay a baby-sitter to watch the twins while the other kids are in school. And what will I do when Aunt Louise go back to work?"

Mama kept rambling on until Aunt Pearl stopped her.

"I don't know what else you can do except..." Aunt Pearl was interrupted by Mama.

"How about if I cleaned a few more houses on the

weekend, like you're doing now?" Mama asked.

"Well, I'll check around. There's always someone who needs their summer home cleaned around the lake."

I knew Aunt Pearl would be able to find someone. Our family argued and didn't agree on everything, but we made sure to help each other not starve.

* * *

It was four weeks later, Mama called all of us kids into the house. Mike and Edward came running from behind the chicken coop. I ran into the house, playing with Tuffy, and Thomas came out of the boys' bedroom.

Instead of going to the dining room table, Mama asked us to sit in the living room.

Mama sat in her chair next to the front door. At first she didn't say anything, just smiled. We looked at each other wondering what was going on. Mama blurted "I have another job."

"What kind of job?" Mike asked.

"There's not much I'll be hired for here in White Cloud, but two things." Mama hesitated before saying, "I'll be cleaning houses with Aunt Pearl on Saturday mornings, you know around the lake. Some houses have to be opened before the owners arrive. And working Aunt Louise' shift at the facility until she heals."

"Whose houses?" we asked.

Mama waited to answer. "One house will be the Gunning house."

"What!" I yelled.

The Gunning house was well-known in the community. It sat on a hill with a long stairway leading down to the lake. The Gunnings didn't like coloreds.

"What is the other job?" Edward asked.

"This summer, we'll all be picking crops in—"

"What!" the four of us yelled at once.

"The crops in our backyard?" Joe asked.

"No, stupid," I said. "Other people's crops."

"Don't you ever let me hear you call your brothers or sister stupid, do you understand me?" Mama said.

I jerked backward on the couch. "Yes, ma'am."

"Yes ma'am what?"

"Yes ma'am I understand."

"There'll be more information later on, but, for now, this is what has to happen."

Thomas and Edward left the living room and walked to their room. Mike turned on the TV for the twins.

While Mama sat on the front steps, facing the Harris' field across the road. I went outside and sat on the top step at the back of the house with nothing to listen to but the cows, chickens, and goat.

I understood Mama cleaning houses, that's how grandma made her living. But picking crops? I was mad. Furious.

Ever since Daddy had left, things got worse and worse. Our family was poorer than poor.

"Hey, young lady!" Uncle Ted waved to me from across the yard.

I leaped up from the steps and followed him into his wood shed. Uncle Ted used the wood shed to store his saws, fixed things around the land and houses. Upstairs was an apartment that was rented out from time-to-time.

"You sure do like to saw a lot," I said, eyeing the saws that were stored in the shed.

"Well, it's something I learned, trying to make money around here. And, since none of us can afford to hire anybody,

I help take care of our own. People know different things, and this is what I know."

"What do you mean when you say 'our own'?"

"Family. Like right now, I'm looking to see if I have enough material to fix our roof. It rained and the water leaked into the bathroom."

"We have several leaks in our front room. We put out buckets to catch the rain."

"I wonder why your mama didn't say anything sooner," Uncle Ted said as he wandered around his shed.

Both Uncle Ted and Uncle John helped our family fix whatever needed to be repaired. They also showed my brothers how to chop wood and wrap pipes for the winter.

As I walked around Uncle Ted's shed and listened to him tell me about family, I began to understand.

The seven of us lived in our two-bedroom house in the middle of a rural community where jobs weren't plentiful. But, no matter what, Mama made sure we had food on the table and clothes on our backs. And, although I didn't like the decision to pick crops, it was a family vote.

Chapter 4

When our families moved here from Baldwin, the first church we became members of was the Baptist church two miles from our house. Every Sunday, for nearly a year, we sat in the first two rows.

But, it was on a cool evening at a Saturday dinner at Uncle Ted and Aunt Louise's house the adults began to talk about a White Cloud Church in Christ, located on the east side of town, I was surprised. Over the time we've attended the church up the road, there hadn't been talk of leaving.

"The congregation is smaller," Uncle Ted said. He ate a spoonful of mashed potatoes. "But the church could fit 100 people or more if chairs were put in the aisles on both sides."

"How did you hear about this church?" Mama asked.

"I was sitting in my office at the courthouse when a man knocked on the door and asked for directions to the city clerk's office. I passed him later in the hallway and he invited me to attend this church."

"Did you go?" Mama asked.

"I attended one of their night services during the middle of the week. "The only way I can explain it was that I felt comfortable. More so than at the church we've been attending." Uncle Ted picked up his cup of coffee.

Everyone at the adult table glanced at each other and without asking for a vote, they nodded. That was confirmation. Of course, the kids didn't have a say. We just followed along with whatever was decided.

At home that night, Mama came out from our bedroom and said, "Mike, Edward, and Thomas, you boys need to make sure your dress shirts are ironed for church tomorrow. Maggie, you can wear your white blouse and black pleated skirt."

The boys ironed their shirts and ties. Mama ironed her favorite dress—a pink one with pretty flowers.

I slowly ironed my blouse and every pleat of that darn skirt. The skirt was more attractive once all the twenty pleats were ironed the right way, but I hated ironing it.

"Mike," Mama said, "make sure the iron is shut off and unplugged. At nine o'clock, everyone should be in bed."

At seven the next morning, I woke up to the smell of bacon, eggs, and toast. I stretched my arms and moved away part of the "night rag" that had moved over the top of my face. The night rag is an old, small shear scarf used to hold our hair and rollers in place. All of the women in our family wore them.

Everyone had taken baths last night, so all we had to do this morning was wash our faces and brush our teeth. The boys were first. Mary and I went second. Mama waited patiently and went last. She figured it took her less time to get ready than the rest of us kids. This also gave her time to read Scripture and to count her change to put in the church offering.

Mary wasn't kindergarten age and slow, so at times, Mama asked me to help her dress. While I was helping Mary put on her shoes, Mama was in the bathroom us and combing her hair. She looked out the bathroom window and noticed the boys walking out the driveway.

"Maggie!" she said. "Go and stop your brothers from walking up the road. Hurry up. They're almost out the driveway."

"Mike. Thomas. Edward," I hollered with my hands cupped around my mouth. "Mama said come back."

Thomas bumped into Mike and Edward. Tuffy was wagging his tail, jumping up and down.

"What?" Mike said.

"Come back."

"Why?" Mike yelled. "Just come back."

When everyone was dressed Mama told us to get into the car without getting dirty and wait for her. At the same time, Uncle John and Aunt Pearl's car pulled into the driveway.

"Before you get in that car, don't forget to tie that dog up," Uncle Ted reminded the boys while walking out of his house. "Last time he smelled horribly of skunk. He was probably bothering one."

Mike caught Tuffy and tied him to the big oak tree near his dog house.

My family and relatives drove down the road as if we were in a parade. Uncle Ted drove the lead car and passed the Baptist church's entrance. We were the second car, followed by Uncle John and Aunt Pearl in the last car.

Twenty minutes later, we drove into a church's swampy parking lot. It had a huge apple tree next to it. Big white letters were painted on the highest point of the church: White Cloud Church of God in Christ.

The parking lot was full. We followed Uncle Ted to the back parking lot and parked next to each other. I noticed my best friend's house on the other side of the fence.

Uncle Ted walked to the front of the church and opened

the church door. Uncle John and Aunt Pearl followed him. Our family went in last.

A person approached Uncle Ted. "Praise God," he said. "My name is Deacon Martin. Thank you for extending my invitation."

"Yes," Uncle Ted said. "Let me introduce my family."

"Praise God, everyone," Deacon Martin said after Uncle Ted introduced us. "I'll give your family a quick tour. As you can see, this is our sanctuary." He pointed. "More members are on their way, and church will begin shortly."

There were two large stained glass windows on each side of the church near the front. I was mesmerized and studied them. Jesus was in the middle. He knelt on one knee, hands folded, praying. The tall ceiling had two big water stains in the corner.

Why can't Jesus fix the water stains, and why can't he answer Mama's prayers? I thought. In an instant, I remembered Mama teaching me to never question Jesus, and begged his pardon.

Music came from a corner of the church. A heavyset lady played the piano, and two people stood next to her, one slouched on the piano, singing.

"Oh. That's Sister Rose, the choir director," Deacon Martin said. "Our choir sings every Sunday, unless there is a concert with a choir from another church. Then both church choirs sing."

We walked through the kitchen. It smelled like home.

"There are Sundays that our church serves lunch. We eat as one big family, and it allows people to stay for the night service instead of having to drive home and then back."

The Deacon opened the kitchen's screen door and asked where we had parked our cars.

Uncle Ted pointed. "Right there. All three cars."

"Thank you for following the parking signs. Normally, there is plenty of room in the main parking lot, but today another church has joined our service," Deacon Martin said. After he had given us a tour of the church, he led our family back to the sanctuary. "I'll leave you here in the capable hands of our ushers. I have to tend to the pastor. Again, welcome."

Two ushers, one male and one female, turned and greeted us with smiles. The man wore a black suit, white shirt, and black tie. The woman wore a white dress suit, pantyhose, and black pumps. They each wore white gloves.

The male usher shook Uncle Ted's hand. "Welcome," he said. "Please follow me."

The other usher shook hands with the rest of us. Her warm, soft smile made me feel like she already knew our family.

After we were seated, I leaned around Mike and looked back at the usher. She gave me another smile.

We sat in the second row from the back on wooden folding chairs, just like the ones at the Baptist church we attended.

While the rest of the congregation walked to their seats, I looked around the church again.

The choir was lined up at the back of the church, females on one side and males on the other, wearing black and white. I figured black and white was the theme for today.

Deacon Martin stood at the front of the church and asked everyone to rise.

The pastor walked through a door from the back of the pulpit. Three other pastors stood.

"Mike, who are the men standing up there?" I asked.

"I don't know. Someone will probably introduce them later."

The pastor knelt at his seat to pray and then sat in the

middle chair. Immediately, the choir director stood up from the piano and signaled the choir to begin singing. They marched down the middle aisle into the choir stand. I noticed Kathy when she passed our row. She went to my school.

"Mama," I whispered. "That's—"

"Shhh," Mama said.

When the pastor gave his sermon, saying all of his "hallelujahs", I found myself listening to almost every word. There was something different about this pastor. For the first time, Mama didn't have to tell me to follow the Scripture.

Uncle Ted was right. There was a certain warmth. I had a sense of calmness that I hadn't felt before.

The next Sunday our family visited the White Cloud Church of God in Christ for the second time. Uncle Ted and Aunt Louise sat closer to the front with Uncle John and Aunt Pearl. For some reason, Mama and our family, again, sat near the back. I was leaning my head against Mike's shoulder and heard a loud "Amen."

Pastor Johnson was standing behind the pulpit with both arms raised. "Is there anyone who'd like to come up for prayer?"

Two people from the congregation got up from their seats and walked together to the front of the church.

The pastor came around the pulpit and laid his hands on both of their heads. The congregation stood and began to pray. The echoes from their prayers filled the church.

Once everyone sat down, Pastor Johnson paced back and forth before stopping behind the pulpit. "This is the time in our service where we ask if anyone would like to join our church, the White Cloud Church of God in Christ. If there is anyone who would like to join and become part of our family, please come forward."

The choir director played soft music while the choir

sung. People in the church prayed, but no one walked forward. Then Mama stood up slowly and said, "The Dorsey family would like to join."

I opened my mouth in surprise.

Mama grabbed my little sister's hand and gestured for Mike, Edward, Thomas, Joe, and me to stand. We followed her to the pulpit.

"Please, everyone gather around," Pastor Johnson said.

Soon, Uncle Ted, Aunt Louise, Uncle John, and Aunt Pearl got up from their seats and joined our family at the altar.

"Today," Uncle Ted said, "our entire family would like to join.

More claps and "hallelujahs". The congregation gathered around our family and blessed us into the White Cloud Church of God in Christ.

Pastor Johnson smiled at us. "Later this summer, your family, along with others, will be baptized up the road in the White River. Deacon Martin can help you with that process."

From then on, our family was raised in the Church of God in Christ, or COGIC some called it, faith. Mama made sure all of us kids joined the Young People Christian Council (YPCC) and Young People Willing Workers (YPWW).

My brothers, sister, and I were in every Christmas and Easter play, and met our quota for the church's largest fundraiser, selling chicken dinners every summer. Since there were six of us, we sold a lot of chicken dinners.

It seemed like we were at church as often as we were at school. No matter what our facial expressions were, this was something that became our custom.

Chapter 5

Pastor Johnson lived across the road but was sick. The assistant pastor, Pastor Adams, and his family lived in Flint, Michigan. The church doors were unlocked at nine o'clock and Sunday School still started an hour later. As usual, our family's three cars paraded into the parking lot.

One of the best things about attending the church was that Cheryl, my best friend, lived next door. Cheryl and I had been best friends since kindergarten. Through our friendship, our mamas became closer. Sometimes they visited each other.

I counted the hours and then minutes until the pastor finished preaching. Today not only was he long-winded, but after service, the line for prayer reached to the back of the church. Once the last person received prayer and Pastor Adams dismissed the congregation.

No matter how many times I'd try to sneak out of the church after services to see Cheryl, I heard Mama's voice. "Remember to wipe the seats in the sanctuary and choir stand."

There were twenty rows on each side of the church and

six rows in the choir stand. Mike and Edward were responsible for the seats in the sanctuary. Thomas and I the choir stand.

"Stop sitting in the chairs and get busy," Mike hollered. "It's only six rows."

Thomas and I stood up. We looked at each other. "I'll race you," I said.

"How?" Thomas asked.

"You start at the back row, and I'll start right here near the wall. We have three rows each. Let's see who can finish first."

Thomas smiled and nodded, like he was winning. He began to move forward, one hand on top of the seat and the other against the back.

"On your mark, get set..." I edged to the tip of the seat. "Go." I whispered, so only Thomas could hear.

By the time I was at the end of my first row, Thomas had begun his second row. He stumbled and grabbed onto the chair in the next row. I caught up with him.

I gave him a bragging smile, two seats from the last one. I reached for the seat and wiped it. Then Mike startled me by hollering, "Stop playing around up there."

Thomas raised his last seat.

"Darn it," I said.

"Ha, ha. I won."

"This time."

Thomas and I walked from the choir stand, bumping each other.

"You two can help us with the rest of the seats in the front," Mike said.

A few minutes later, Uncle Ted came into the sanctuary. "Are all of the seats ready?"

"We're on our last two rows," Mike said.

Uncle Ted kept walking, jiggling his keys inside his

pocket. He didn't hold an official title, but church members called him Brother McKinney.

Five minutes after he unlocked the doors, members gathered into the sanctuary. They hugged each other, said, "God bless you," and prayed for Pastor Johnson's speedy recovery.

The deacons sat along the side of the church near the pulpit. Five seats with white cloth hung over the back were reserved for the mothers and missionaries of the church. The seats next to them were for the pastor and assistant pastor's families.

The assistant pastor also had a reserved parking space near the back of the church. One of the deacons met him in his office. The missionaries and church members gathered in the church until the deacon came from the pastor's office.

"Could everyone please stand?" the deacon asked.

Members stood while the music played. With Pastor Johnson sick, Mother Johnson stayed home. Their daughter came to church and sat in the chair reserved for her. Sister Adams, the assistant pastor's wife, and their children came and sat in their seats. A church nurse stood nearby.

Soon after, Assistant Pastor Adams opened his office door. He always had the kindest smile, like his world was perfect, without problems.

But pastors must have problems, too, I reasoned. It couldn't be that easy driving back and forth every Sunday, and sometimes during the week, helping to pastor a half-full church. He must get tired. And how did his children feel when they left the city to come to a countrified church with the smell of chickens, pigs, and horse manure in the surrounding area?

The choir lined up in the back of the church. When the choir director waved her hand, they began to walk down the middle aisle, singing a song by one of my favorite gospel singers, Mahalia Jackson.

My eyes followed them as they swayed side-to-side in unison, with the exception of one boy. The choir moved one way and he moved the other until the person behind him touched his shoulders, getting him to sway in the same direction.

I snickered. Edward bumped me.

When the choir reached their seats, the choir director announced, "Today, the choir will sing one selection. Please clap along if you like what you hear."

A girl from the choir walked to the piano. The choir director handed her a mic.

When they finished singing, the testimonial service began. Forty-five minutes later, Assistant Pastor Adams stood. After he led the congregation in prayer for Pastor Johnson, he said, "Could everyone please turn to Joshua, first chapter, verses one through nine?"

I thumbed through the pages of the Bible, not sure where to find Joshua. Edward elbowed me. "As much as Mama makes us read the Bible, you can't find Joshua?"

Mama leaned forward, frowning. She put her finger up to her mouth.

"Will you two be quiet?" Mike said. "Hand me your Bible, Maggie."

Assistant Pastor Adams read from the Bible with passion. He enunciated his words perfectly, pacing behind the pulpit. He asked us to repeat verses after him and said, "Hallelujah" and "Amen."

After the last "Amen," I leaned against Edward. Slowly, I closed my eyes, opening them each time the congregation reacted to what the assistant pastor said.

Edward nudged me with his shoulder. I must have drifted off to sleep. People in the congregation were jumping up and down, hollering, "Thank you, Jesus!" and "Hallelujah!" Even Mama was shouting and praising the Lord. The piano music was so loud.

Gradually, the congregation became calm, the shouting turning to murmurs. Someone fanned Mama until she sat down.

In all our time at the Baptist church, I had never seen Mama shouting for Jesus. But it was all right. She was at peace.

"What time is it?" I asked Edward.

"Three thirty."

I stood and straightened my dress. Mama looked at us. "We're all going to eat in the kitchen today. Evening service starts soon after, so don't go far."

We all sighed, except for the twins. Neither one of them were paying attention.

The line to eat began at the entrance of the kitchen door. It moved slowly. I sat in the chairs along the wall where the deacons sat during the service. As the line moved, I sat in a different chair until there was no place to sit. It made me miss the Baptist church that was near our house. If we were still going there, we'd be home by now, changed out of our Sunday clothes instead of standing in a line waiting to eat and then going to another service.

The tables were full of fried chicken, mashed potatoes, fried corn bread, collard greens, drinks, and desserts.

"Don't put more on your plate than you can eat, Maggie," Mama said. "Mike, would you fix the twins' plates?"

"Okay," Mike said.

I looked at Mike with a softness. He took on large role watching over us kids with very little complaints.

"That's all right Mike," I said. "Here, Mary, you can have my plate."

"Can I sit next to you, too?" she asked.

"Sure."

Even with our difference in age, she not in kindergarten, I loved my sister and liked having her around.

"Maggie?" Mary said quietly. "You know your walking doll, the one in the corner at home?"

"Yes."

"Do you mind if I play with her sometimes?"

I hadn't known she paid any attention to that old doll. I was six years old when Daddy gave it to me. A Christmas catalogue had come in the mail, and I remember ripping the page out to show the doll to Daddy. He must had hidden the doll in the attic and waited for Christmas to give it to me.

The doll had rubber bands on its feet. I placed the rubber bands underneath mine. Daddy played his music and we'd dance until I was exhausted.

Being the only girl for a long time among three boys, I wanted someone to talk to, and my doll, Lilly, became like my little sister. I'd sit in the clothes closet with her and talk about anything and everything.

During the past two years, I had stopped talking to Lilly and tucked her in the corner between the dresser and attic door. Now the doll no longer had rubber bands on her feet and her clothes were dingy. It brought back memories when Mary asked for my doll, but it was time to let someone else enjoy her.

"You can play with her," I said. "Do you want to keep her? I don't play with her anymore."

Mary hopped up and down in her chair as if Christmas was here.

A dog barking caught my attention. Cheryl was outside feeding chickens.

I looked at Mary, not wanting to mess up our sisterly moment, but also wanting to rush over to Cheryl. "Mary, are you almost done eating?" I asked.

"Yeah," she answered.

"My best friend lives next door. Do you want to come with me or stay here with Joe?" I asked.

"Well, I do want some cake?"

"Save me a piece?" I kissed Mary on the cheek and ran to the screen door.

Every Sunday for the past month, I sat at the same table after church service wanted to run over to Cheryl's house and let her know about our family joining the church. There wasn't any rhyme or reason why I hadn't told her yet. But, decided I would today.

"Where you going?" Mama's voice stopped me in my tracks.

"Outside to talk with Cheryl."

"What about your sister?"

"She's eating cake with Joe."

"Don't be long. Night service starts soon."

"Cheryl! Cheryl!" I yelled.

The chickens' clucks grew louder as they scattered around to peck at the feed, distracting Cheryl.

I called her name again and again, running closer to the fence, until she looked up.

"What you doin' over here? Visiting the church again?"

"Guess what?" I said.

"I don't know."

"My family joined the church."

Cheryl screamed. "You're lying."

"No. The whole family."

Both of us jumped up and down. The chickens scattered even more, and Cheryl's dog barked louder. He ran back and forth along the fence, wagging his tail. Cheryl told him to shut up.

Mama yelled, "Are you guys all right?" She stood by

the church kitchen's screen door. "I heard the dog."

"Yeah," I yelled back. "He's barkin' for no reason."

"So," Cheryl said, "we can see each other every Sunday?"

"Yep," I said.

Unless there were church visitors or we left to visit another church, Cheryl and I met at the fence or climbed the apple tree in the backyard of the church.

Chapter 6

Pastor Johnson had recovered from his illness and resumed his pastoral role. He walked down from the pulpit and sat two seats away from Mama. "During my absence, I learned that you have many talents."

"What do you mean, Pastor?" Mama asked.

"I've been told, now correct me if I'm wrong, that you can play the piano and sing."

Our family was sitting in the second row, behind Mama. We all leaned forward in our seats and made eye contact with each other.

"Sister Martin and I met after the service a few Sundays ago in the church office. She told me that she and her family will be moving out of the county. I'm wondering if you wouldn't mind assuming the role of church choir director."

Pastor Johnson walked back up to the pulpit.

"I have an announcement," he said. "Sister Martin, the current choir director, has informed me that she and her husband will be moving from White Cloud, excuse me, the county. He has accepted a better paying job."

The congregation clapped, saying, "Thank you, Jesus."

Pastor Johnson paused. "The pastors have decided that there is among us a very capable person to not replace Sister Martin, but to add to our flock as choir director."

Murmurs ran rampant through the church, everyone wondering.

"Sister Dorsey, please stand."

The entire congregation stood, clapped loudly, and smiled at Mama, which made my family smile even more.

I had harbored concern that the church didn't accept Mama. I quickly learned that if the pastor says it's okay, then everyone is accepting.

Mama bowed to the congregation and said, "Thank you for your support." Then she turned back around. "And thank you, choir. I'll see you at four o'clock for a brief meeting."

Mama sat down. She leaned back in her seat and turned to my brothers and me. "That means all of you Dorseys, too."

My brothers and sister half smiled. I crossed my arms, frowning.

Our first choir practice was held after everyone had a chance to eat. Deacon Martin interrupted our practice. "Sister Dorsey," he whispered. "Pastor Johnson would like to see you in his office."

"Let's take a five-minute break," Mama said, "but don't go out of the church sanctuary."

She went into Pastor Johnson's office which was next to the choir stand. The door was cracked open. Some of the choir members went to the bathroom. Two other members and I stayed in our seats talking.

"Praise the Lord, Pastor. You wanted to see me."

"Praise the Lord to you too, Sister Dorsey. I hear the choir. How is it going? Smoothly, I pray."

"Shhh," I said. "Listen."

"On short notice, the choir seems to be adjusting to my style. I haven't heard any complaints yet. Are you happy with the song selections you've heard?"

"All of the songs are great. Everyone is singing on key and sounds soulful. The reason I wanted to see you is the practices won't all flow over into our night service or YPWW time, will they?"

"Well, Pastor, I've been thinkin'. How about holding practices at my house on a Saturday?"

Pastor Johnson rocked back in his chair. "Well, Sister Dorsey, if it's okay with the parents and adults, then it's okay with me. But keep the practices shorter than they are at the church. Practice can be held here, if there's time."

Mama came back from the pastor's office. "Choir, please come back to the choir stand."

Everyone sat in the same seats before Mama's meeting.

"I have an announcement," Mama said. "From time-to-time, practices will be held at my house on Saturday afternoons. The first rehearsal will be this Saturday at three o'clock."

* * *

I was jumping rope in the driveway, counting my jumps, when a car honked. It startled me. I dropped the rope and turned around. It was Mama.

She stuck her head out the window. "Move out of the way."

As she drove closer to the back door, I ran alongside the car. "Mama, you're home early."

"How many times did you jump this time?" she asked.

When the car stopped, I leaned against it for support. "Fifty times. Twenty-five more than the last time." I wiped sweat off my forehead.

"Child, you always challenge yourself. Do you have a goal you're trying to reach before those string-bean legs are too wobbly to walk?"

"I'm not sure."

"Where are your brothers?"

"Mike and Edward are behind the chicken coop playing basketball. Thomas is...Thomas is inside."

Darn it, I thought.

"Who's watching the twins?"

I rolled my eyes, trying to think what to say. "Well..." The sweat rolled down my face. "Thomas."

"Thomas!" Mama repeated with a concerned look. "Move so that I can get out of this car."

Thomas wasn't the best at watching himself, let alone someone else. But Mike and Edward felt he needed to take on more responsibility and had asked him to watch the twins for a while. He had argued, but the two older brothers grabbed onto his arms and forced him. Mama wasn't supposed to know.

"It was Mike's idea," I said.

"Mike!" Mama hollered.

Mike and Edward came running from behind the chicken coop, bouncing their basketball, their faces concerned. No one had expected Mama to be home so early.

I was concerned for my own life for telling.

"You left Thomas to watch the twins?" Mama asked.

"It wasn't for long," Mike said.

Mama and the rest of us hurried into the house.

She called out his name. "Thomas!"

He rushed out of his bedroom.

Mary and Joe ran from the living room into Mama's arms, nearly knocking her over.

"Are you guys all right?" she asked.

"Yeah. Thomas is a good baby-sitter. He let us do whatever we wanted, Joe said."

"No fighting, I hope."

"Oh no, Mama." The twins continued to hug her. "He told us that was forbidden."

Mama pulled the twins away from her. "Are you sure?" She turned around to make sure Thomas wasn't helping them answer.

"Yes."

Mama walked into the bedroom that Mary, she, and I shared. I followed her.

"Maggie, one moment," she said. "Now, tell me all about your day."

As soon as I got out another three words, Mama stopped me again. "I'm sorry, Maggie. Give me ten minutes and let me slip out of this dress. Then I promise you can tell me all about everything you did today, okay?"

Mama had gotten home at one o'clock this afternoon, plenty of time for me to ask if I can go to Cheryl's house until Thomas called my name.

"Maggie," Thomas called. "Do you wanna play checkers?"

I didn't answer.

"Maggie."

"Thomas..."

"Oh, sweetie, go and play one game," Mama said. "We can talk as soon as I come from the bedroom."

Thomas and I sat at the table, the board already set up. He chose the black chips.

"You can move first," Thomas said.

I moved my chips and he moved his. Thomas was a very good player, the best of all us kids. Nearing the end of the game, he continually tapped his chips against the table. I was about to make a move. Not only was Thomas a good player, he loved to distract you.

"Stop making that noise," I said.

"Nervous?"

I moved my chip from one square to the other across the board and shouted. "Ha. Your noise diversion didn't work. I still won and we've played one game. "

"Let's play another one."

I scooted my chair from the table when Thomas spoke up. "Mama's not gonna let you go."

"What are you talkin' about?"

"You're tryin' to spend the night with Cheryl, aren't you?" he said.

"How did you know?"

"Don't worry about how I know," he answered.

"The only person I mentioned this to was," I paused. Edward. He can't keep a secret to save his soul. "I don't care what you think you know, I need to speak to Mama."

The pastor's daughter lived across the road from the church and had become friends with Cheryl and me. We talked about boys and walked up the road to Mr. Anderson's house to ride his horses. That was the plan for today. The choir had already practiced this week, so I didn't see why I wouldn't be able to go.

Mama passed the table and caught me by surprise.

"Mama—"

Her eyes were focused on one thing: the refrigerator door. She ran her finger down the list of chores taped to it. "Mike," she called.

"Yes, ma'am."

"I see that you switched chores with Maggie again. Is there a reason that Maggie can't cook?"

"No. I thought that since I do most of the cooking

anyway, she could do my cleaning. Besides, she might burn herself or burn the house down."

"You're going to spoil that girl. What will she do when she grows up and gets married and the man finds out she can't cook?"

"She'll probably learn by then."

"I'm headed over to Aunt Louise's house. I'll be back shortly. And Mike, since you like to cook so much and it's really Maggie's week, could you get supper ready?" She smiled at him and walked to the door.

I hurried to stop her and pushed my chair under the table, scraping it against our floor. She stopped. The annoying sound caught Mama's attention.

Thomas laughed as I stumbled to the floor. "Mama? Can I please spend Saturday night at Cheryl's house? I can take my church clothes and meet everyone at church."

"We have an additional choir practice tomorrow. I'm sorry. Maybe another time." Mama walked out the door. She left for Aunt Louise' house.

I plopped on the stool next to the rotary phone, dialing each number. "Cheryl, I'm sorry, but I can't come over tonight. Mama said maybe another one."

I sighed and slammed the phone down on the receiver. The twins flinched. They turned around to look at me but didn't say a word. I slumped my shoulders and fell down onto the lumpy couch, crossing my arms.

"What you watchin'?" I asked.

"Adam, um —" Mary hesitated to think.

"Twelve, knucklehead," Thomas said.

A drop of water hit my forehead. When I looked up, I saw another leak in the ceiling.

"Mama won't let you go over to your friend's house, eh?" Edward leaned through the opening in the wall between the kitchen and living room.

"Ha. Ha," I responded back.

"Well, you'll have plenty of company tomorrow when the choir members come here."

I frowned and then stuck out my tongue at him.

"Don't you have anything better to do than bother Maggie?" Mike asked Edward. "Now move so I can start supper."

I got on my knees on the couch and looked through the opening between the kitchen and living room to see what Mike was preparing. He had pulled the big black skillet from the cupboard and a can of lard. Then he opened the refrigerator and reached for the pan of uncooked chicken that was already seasoned.

"If you're gonna watch, you might as well come and help," Mike said. "Here, come and mix the chicken in this bag of flour. Then squeeze the bag shut and shake the chicken up and down."

I shook the bag. Flour came from a crack at the bottom.

"That's all right," he said. "Now lay the chicken in the frying pan slowly. I don't want you to burn yourself and have Mama get the belt after me."

Usually, I hated to cook, but Mike made it seem kind of fun.

"Stand back from the stove," he said, "or you'll get burned."

"Forget that she'll get burned," Edward said. "What about the food?"

"Leave her alone. At least she's cookin'," Mike said.

While we waited for the chicken to fry, Mike asked me to help with the string beans. "A canned jar should be in the lower cupboard."

Fresh sweet corn that we had shucked earlier today

was already boiling in a pan on the stove. While the food was cooking, Mike was able to sit at the dining room table. He double checked the list of chores.

I sat next to him.

"I know that you want to visit your friends. Next weekend will be here before you know it."

"Yeah," I said somberly.

"You run around after us boys anyway. And Cousin Sonya and Jeffrey will be coming up from Chicago. You can hang out with them this summer."

He was right, but I still wanted to see my friends too.

The back door squeaked.

"Hey, Mama. Dinner's almost ready, and you won't be able to guess who helped."

Mama walked to the kitchen, but paused. "Mary helped?" She smiled.

"No, Mama, I helped," I said.

"I was joking. That's good, sweetheart. You're headed in the right track."

"Maybe."

"Do you mind setting the table with Mary? I'll check the food."

While Mary and I set the table, Mama and Mike put the string beans in a bowl and the fried chicken on a platter.

"Let's bow our heads for grace," Mama said. "Thomas, it's your turn."

Uh-oh, I thought.

"Lord, thank you for this food and...Let's eat."

"Thomas," Mama said, "I tell you every time, you need to be more thankful to the Lord for any food we eat. God's been good to us. Tomorrow you'll have another turn blessing the food, and hopefully you'll be a little more thankful."

Unless Mama had something to tell us kids, the

beginning of dinner was the quietest time in our house. There were just the slurping of Kool-Aid, spoons and forks clanking against plates, and the twins fussing.

"Mary and Joe," Mama said. "Why do you two always have to fuss and kick each other under the table?"

They shrugged their shoulders. "I don't know." Then they smiled.

Mama got up from her chair, walked into the kitchen, and removed the towel from one of the pies. "I hope these pies can last through the weekend," she said, looking at Thomas.

Thomas was a year younger than me but ate like he was a grown man. Mama always told him that he ate so much that food was going to grow out of his head. We'd laugh. Tuffy would bark outside by the door, probably for his meal.

When Mama got back to the table, she said, "As you know, every summer we..."

I thought. Here it comes.

We slumped down in our chairs before Mama could finish her sentence.

"Every summer we work one or two different fields. We've decided this year that we'll top onions on the other side of White Cloud. And...we start on Monday."

For once, I thought, why can't we play at the beach like the white kids and hang around with our cousins?

"Mama," I said, "what about your job in Fremont, and cleaning houses, and welfare? With all of that, we still have to work in the fields?"

"Be quiet, Maggie!" Mike said.

"I'm sorry," I said. "The words just blurted out of my mouth." Most times, they did.

My eyes got teary. "I didn't mean to say that and..."

She kept staring at me, not saying a word.

Mama wiggled her finger and said, "Let me tell you

something, young lady. Sometimes, I believe you have lost your mind. I always tell you to think before you speak. Our whole family is doing the best we can. No one likes topping the white man's onions, but for now, that's what we have to do."

She scooted her chair away from the table. "I love all of you, but, until you're able to provide for yourselves, and while you're living under my roof, this is what all of us have to do."

We lowered our heads and said quietly, "Yes, ma'am."

The room was solemn when Mama left and walked into the bedroom.

Mike, Edward, and Thomas glared at me. "You always gotta say something, don't you?" They pushed their chairs back and took their plates into the kitchen.

Mary lingered behind. "I'll help you, Maggie. You can dry the dishes and I'll wash them." She couldn't reach the sink and stood on the footstool.

"Be careful not to break anything, okay?" I said.

After the last pot was dried and put in the cupboard, I moved the curtain on the railing to the bedroom that Mama, Mary, and I shared. Mama was sitting on the edge of the bed reading her Bible.

I sat next to her and folded my hands in my lap, rubbing them with my head held down. "Mama, I am really, really sorry. I pray every night that you won't have to work so hard. I know you don't like working those fields either, and..."

Mama laid her hand on top of mine. I stopped talking for a minute, and our eyes met.

"It just feels like we're field hands," I continued. "I know you like to say we're picking crops because we're going to make money, and sometimes the farmers let us bring some of the crops home. But Mama, the other kids who top onions call us field hands."

"It don't matter what they call you or me. What matters

is that we make an honest living to help put food on the table and have a little for gas and clothes for you kids' backs." Mama caressed her Bible. "Child, you have a lot of growing up to do. I accept your apology, not because you apologized, but because you didn't take until the next day to do it."

I reached to hug her.

Mama always told us kids, "Never go to bed mad or upset. It's always good to sleep with a positive mind. It helps you have good dreams."

The next day, Saturday afternoon, Mama washed and braided Mary's hair. While she was pressing my hair with the hot comb, Tuffy started to bark outside.

Mike ran to the bathroom window to see what the commotion was all about. "Mama, cars are pullin' up in the driveway. Looks like some of the choir members!" he hollered.

"Go and get that dog," Mama told Mike. "Hurry, Maggie, go and get your rag to wrap around your head. I'll put the rollers in it later tonight."

Mike hurried to the door. One by one, the choir members came in, smiling. They hugged, saying, "Praise the Lord, Sister and Brother."

Mama greeted the members. Then she sat at the piano until Don, our neighbor, came through the door. He was the choir's piano player. He never had any formal training but could play anything by listening.

People talked and ate the snacks Mama had prepared.

Don sat down at the piano, tapping one key and then another. I sat next to him as he sang a melody.

"You try," he told me. "Hit this white key."

I tapped the key.

"Don't be afraid of the keys. Think of them as your friends." He sang a note. "Now touch this key right here."

"That doesn't sound like your voice," I said.

"You're right. Now touch this key."

The key sounded just like his voice. "Why can't I learn to play the piano like you instead of taking boring piano lessons?"

"This works for me, but you better listen to your mama and continue to take those lessons."

"Maybe."

"Okay, let's try again."

He sang a melody and placed his fingers over mine, helping me along the way.

Ten minutes later, Mama said, "Could everyone please stand in their spots?"

Choir members stepped in between each other until everyone was in their right position. I stood in front of Edward.

"Okay," Mama said. "The first song is 'Go, Tell It on the Mountain." She extended her arms halfway and nodded at Don—his signal to begin playing. "Choir, follow my hand directions."

Everyone but Lucy moved from left to right.

"Everyone, please stop," Mama said. "Let's try this again. Follow my hand directions and move left to right."

She asked Don to stop playing and told us not to sing. She held Lucy by the shoulders and moved her in the same directions as the rest of the choir. "Do you think you have it now?"

Lucy nodded and smiled.

"Okay, let's start from the beginning," Mama said.

The choir moved in the same direction as Mama. This time no one bumped into each other.

Mama pointed at me. I hated singing the lead, but for some reason, Mama felt it was the godly thing for me to do.

"Don, stop playing," Mama said. "Could you scooch over?"

There were ten people in the choir, and it felt like all of them were staring at me.

"Maggie," Mama said, "you have a beautiful voice, and I know you can sing louder than that. Pretend you're outside running around with your friends at school on the playground. Could you please give me that same loud voice? Sing so the chickens and pigs can hear, so that Tuffy can howl along with you outside."

She turned to show Don something on the piano. Edward jabbed me in the back and whispered in my ear, "Yeah. Sing so the chickens and pigs can hear you."

"Mama, get Edward."

By the time she turned around, Edward stood as if nothing had happened.

"Okay, let's take it from the top," Mama said.

Don began to play, and I sang, "Go, tell it on the mountain, over the hill, and everywhere."

"A little louder, Maggie," Mama said.

"Go, tell it on the mountain that Jesus Christ is born."

"See, I knew you could do it," Mama said.

We rehearsed two songs: one for walking down the center aisle and into the choir stand, and the other for before the pastor's sermon.

"There's something else we have to practice," Mama said. "Your entrance. I've noticed that some of you are rocking in opposite directions."

There was only room for one line. Mama told the boys to get in the back and the girls up front.

Don began playing. We waited for Mama's cue. Her hands went up, and we began to walk but didn't sing.

"That's much better," Mama said. "Choir practice is dismissed."

Voices traveled throughout the house: laughing, joking,

and the boys tussling.

Mama clapped her hands and asked for silence. "Remember to wear black and white. That means black pants, ties, and white shirts for the boys. Girls, wear white blouses and black skirts. Please make sure everything is pressed."

Mama put the choir music in her satchel for tomorrow. I walked beside her. "Do I have to sing in the choir, Mama?" I said, dragging each syllable. "Can I help with something else?"

Mama put her arms around me. "Maggie, you have a beautiful voice, and I'm sure everyone would love to hear it."

"I guess so." I closed the piano cover.

"Go and get your rollers so I can finish your hair. You'll do fine tomorrow."

* * *

After the church service, I ran to Cheryl's backyard. We talked about summer break. Cheryl's father worked every day, and she didn't have to top onions or have any jobs during the summer except around their house.

"What are you doin' this summer?" I asked her.

"Going to Indiana to visit my cousins. I don't know after that. Probably nothing much. What about you?"

"The usual. Toppin' onions." I slumped my shoulders and tossed an apple up and down.

"Well, at least we'll be able to see each other after your church services. I'll be gone only for a few weeks."

"You should visit sometime. You could be my guest at church." I chuckled.

"I'll see." She didn't sound as if I convinced her.

Chapter 7

I was in the middle of a dream with my knight in shining armor. He extended his arm when I slipped on a wet spot on the floor and-

Beep. Beep. Beep. I ignored the sound, pretending I was still asleep.

Mama tapped my legs. "Maggie, don't you hear the alarm clock going off?"

I opened my eyes just enough to see Mama reach for her housecoat and put on her slippers.

Half an hour later, she came back into the bedroom and walked to my side of the bed. "Maggie."

"Huh?"

"Time to get up. The boys are in the bathroom, but you and Mary can go next."

I hated picking crops.

Mary and I put on our housecoats. One of my brothers still in the bathroom. We sat at the dining room table, resting our heads on our arms. It was four-thirty in the morning.

Mike was responsible for the lunches, snacks, and drinks and for putting them in the car. Edward made sure that Tuffy had plenty of food for the day.

Mary and I cuddled up against each other in the car, still tired, and ate our breakfast sandwiches.

"Mike and Edward, are the blankets, sheets, snacks, and lunches packed in the car?" Mama asked.

"Yep. They're in the back," Mike said.

We wore more clothes than needed. It would be chilly until the sun came up.

Aunt Pearl walked down the foot path that was between her house and ours with a flashlight moving around. She yelled, "I'm coming." She stopped at our car. "Remember, I'll be topping onions for the week. John's grandchildren are visiting for the summer."

Aunt Louise honked the horn. "Hurry up, Pearl."

It was last year January, Aunt Louise and Uncle Ted had adopted David. He sat in the backseat of Aunt Louise' car with Mike. David hated going to the fields just as much as us but didn't have a choice either. But it was five-thirty in the morning when Uncle Ted drove out of the driveway. We followed him. The field was ten miles away.

My body moved when Mama stopped at the crossings to turn left to the onion field or right to White Cloud. Uncle Ted flashed his truck lights.

Mama and Aunt Louise honked, which meant for him to have a good day at work. The only interview that Uncle Ted had was janitor at the White Cloud Court House. A week later, he was hired and has worked there ever since.

The onion fields were now five miles away from when Uncle Ted blinked his lights. Within a few miles of the fields, the smell of the onions woke me up. I rubbed my eyes.

Mama was driving on a winding, two-track road.

On each side, trees stood tall, with the top of the branches connecting.

"We're here," Mama said.

The boys opened the back door of our station wagon, got out, and stretched their arms.

I slowly opened the front door. Onions and black muck covered an area further than I could see. Mary and I held our noses.

"Make sure the lid stays on top of the cooler," Mama said. "Otherwise the ice will melt and our drinks will be hot."

"Where do you want me to put the blanket and sheet for Joe and Mary?" Mike asked.

"First, let me see what rows we'll be topping," Mama said.

I stood against our car, staring at the rows and rows of onions. Again this summer, their smell would become part of our bodies.

Ever since I was five years old, I had topped onions, picked apples, cherries, and, for a short time, berries.

"Hurry up, Maggie," Mama said. "The onions won't run to you."

Mama, Aunt Louise, and Aunt Pearl talked to a man who pointed to an area of the field.

"Mike," Mama said, "leave the blankets and sheets in the car for now. It's too early for the twins to be up. Make sure Joe is on the seat and Mary on the front. The family will keep checking on them until they wake up."

Three hours had passed before someone tapped Mike on his shoulder. "Mama," Mike hollered. "It's Mary and Joe."

Mama and Aunt Louise walked to Mike. Each had the hand of one of the twins and put them in the car. They drove their cars up the road in front of the fields where we were topping onions and better shade. Once the cars were parked,

Aunt Pearl spread the blankets and sat with them until lunch time.

Mike, Edward, Thomas, and I had two rows each to top. Large metal shears were used to top and put the onions in the wooden crates that we pulled behind us.

Mike and Edward topped faster than me. "Keep up, Maggie," they'd say.

There wasn't anything to enjoy about topping onions. I paced myself by making up games. I'd walk ten feet and draw a line in between the rows. I'd yell up the row, "Mama what time is it? Is it time to eat?"

She let me wear her watch, telling me not to lose it. I'd race against the clock to be at the line. This annoyed Mama. By lunchtime, it felt like it was ninety degrees. Thank God for hats to keep the sun off our faces.

The best part of our work day was when Mama told my brothers and me that it was time for a break or lunch or to check on Mary and Joe. At least that was a time away from topping onions.

Sometimes I'd say, "I have to go to the bathroom" when I didn't.

Our day was done when the last of the onions in our section were topped.

Mike, Thomas, and I stood against the car. Inside the car, Joe and Mary once again found some way to annoy each other. Edward tossed chunks of muck into the stream of water that rested in between the trees and onion fields.

Mama walked over to the field manager. Aunt Louise and Aunt Pearl joined her.

Later, Mama told us, "We were paid ten cents for every crate that we topped."

No matter how much we were paid, I wasn't happy. I smelled like onions and wanted to go home.

Somehow, during the drive home, I was able to fall asleep. I woke up to Tuffy's barking.

"Mike," Mama said, "you boys let the girls take their bath first because it's only the two of them, unless you boys want to use the hose outside," Mama said.

"I'll wait," Mike said.

"Not us," Edward and Thomas said. "We can put on some shorts."

"Maggie, let me know when you and your sister have finished so that Mike can take his bath," Mama said.

"No, Mama, you can go after them," Mike said. "I'll check the mail and sit on the front porch."

After my bath, I sat on the steps. I was throwing rocks at a spot on the ground when I heard a car honking.

A sparse line of trees separated Uncle John's house and ours. I tried to look between the trees but couldn't see clearly enough. When I heard a second honk, I stood up and walked to the footpath.

I skipped past the trees down the path. A Ford Thunderbird was parked in Uncle John's driveway. I stopped and screamed when my cousins, Sonya and Jeffrey, Uncle John's grandkids, stepped out of the car, stretching. Junior, or "June Bug," as we called him, waved. He was Sonya and Jeffrey's father. This would be the second summer that they visited the granddaddy. Sonya was a year ahead of me and Jeffrey the same age.

"Sonya! Jeffrey!" I yelled.

"Hey, cuz," Sonya and Jeffrey said.

"Let me help you carry your luggage into the house," I said.

Sonya and I plopped down on her bed. We giggled and talked over each other's words.

Aunt Pearl pushed the curtain to the bedroom aside.

"Looks like you guys are happy to see each other,"

"Heck yeah," we said simultaneously.

"Finally, I have someone to play with every day," I said.

"Let Sonya get settled. She can come over in a bit," Aunt Pearl said.

Chapter 8

Today was an off day from topping onions or go to any other fields.

The clothes that Mama and I washed were hanging on the clothesline, swinging back and forth in the afternoon breeze.

Mike and Edward were in the backyard, bouncing the basketball, playing a game of keep away, but with their new rules. When games became boring, the rules were thrown away.

I tossed a rubber ball over Tuffy's head into Mike and Edward's game, but instead of chasing after his ball, Tuffy jumped for the basketball. They stopped and yelled at him. He wouldn't let them play. "Get him out of here, Maggie!" they said.

As Mama walked away from the clothesline, she asked, "What's all that yelling?"

Mike quickly answered, "Nothin', Mama. We're just playin' around."

What the boys were fussing over were the new rules.

The new rule was that Mike could only bounce the ball three times before he had to make the shot.

Edward argued that Mike had bounced the ball four times before making his shot to win the game.

"Why don't you boys stick to the old rules of basketball?" Mama asked.

"This makes it more fun," Edward said.

"Mike just needs to learn the new rule." Edward frowned.

"All I have to say is you boys better stop all that arguing. If you don't, there's plenty of work around here to do," Mama said. "Maggie, it smells like rain and the sky's cloudy. Come help me get everything off the clothesline."

I was close to the clothesline when I saw Cousin Sonya.

"Hey!" She waved.

Cousin Jeffrey wasn't far behind. He smiled and ran to where the boys were playing basketball, but stumbling in the dirt.

"What you up to?" Sonya asked.

"Nothing much. You wanna help me with these?"

"Okay."

Sonya and I grabbed one end of a sheet, giggling and catching up from last year's visit.

"How's Chicago?" I asked.

"The same. Pimps and prostitutes stand on the corners. Daddy's working at the plant. Jeffrey and I are spending most of the summer here, with Granddaddy."

"Dang girl, I only asked about Chicago. Look at those fools." I pointed to Mike and Edward. "Trying to play a game of keep away with Jeffrey. He's taller than both of them."

"Yeah."

A gust of wind took one of the sheets. It tumbled through the air. Sonya and I ran after it until it landed in the bushes behind the shed.

After that, we held the sheets tighter, bundled in our arms.

"Make sure not to lose any clothespins," Mama yelled. "I can't afford to keep buying them."

"Look at Jeffrey," I said to Sonya. "Mike is trying to shoot over him, but I know Jeffrey is gonna swat the ball away."

Mike gave Edward a signal to throw the ball to the side. They knew if it was tossed up high, Jeffrey would catch it.

Edward threw the ball exactly in the direction Mike told him. Jeffrey grabbed the ball and fell to the ground.

Edward was furious because now it was his turn to stand in the middle. He stomped around Jeffrey.

"I don't know why the boys think they can try their sneaky tricks on everyone."

"Jeffrey stumbles over his legs walking, but he's pretty good on the basketball court and this game. The kids in Chicago play it all the time."

Sonya and I, made sure none of the sheets didn't drag on the ground. "Will you guys be picking crops this summer?" I asked Sonya.

She stared down at the ground and didn't answer.

"Sonya, did you hear me?" I touched her arm.

In almost a whisper, she said, "I don't know. Uncle John hasn't said anything."

Why did I ask that question? I thought. In the two years that Sonya and Jeffrey have visited, the only crops I've ever seen them pick are strawberries from Aunt Pearl's garden.

A loud rumbling startled us. We looked up at the sky and rain drops splattered on our faces.

"Go into the house!" Mama yelled.

Sonya and I grabbed the rest of the laundry from

the clothesline and ran inside. Clothespins popped in every direction. The boys ran behind us, nearly pushing Sonya and me over.

"You had better stay inside until the rain stops," Mama said. "I'll call your granddaddy."

Sonya and I folded the sheets and pillowcases and put them on the shelf in the bathroom linen closet. Then we ran through the dining room to one of our favorite spots in the house. I ran around the table one way, and Sonya ran the other way, thinking she'd beat me. She bumped into the table corner and slowed down. I opened the front porch door and plopped down on the oversized chair.

"Stop that running!" Mama hollered from the kitchen.

The only chair left was the hard wooden one. Sonya stood over me with her arms crossed and a sad look on her face.

I scooted over. "There's room enough for the both of us."

"Cousin Louise sure does know how to cook," Sonya said. "It always smells like someone's cooking over here."

The lights flickered from the thunderstorm. I wasn't surprised.

Sonya squeezed my arm.

"It's gonna be all right," I said. "Stay by me."

"Everyone, come into the living room," Mama said. "That means you too, Sonya and Maggie."

"But Mama, we're all right out here."

"Maggie, don't talk back. Everyone should be sitting somewhere in the living room."

Whenever the lights went out, Mike and Edward were responsible for getting the candles from the china cabinet.

Mary leaned against me and squeezed my arm. She was terrified of thunder and scared of the dark.

Most times when the lights went out, we'd tell stories to distract each other from the weather.

"That friend of yours...what's her name?" Sonya asked me. "She lives next door to a church."

"Cheryl. Why do you ask?"

"She seems like a really good person. She treats me like I live here, and not like an outsider."

"What are you talkin' about?"

"Well, sometimes when you have a friend and someone else comes around, friends act differently. Cheryl doesn't."

I think Sonya worried that this year, with everyone getting older, Cheryl might change and not want her around, but there was no way I'd let that happen. After all, Sonya is my cousin.

"Cuz, I haven't heard any thunder in a while," Sonya said.

"And the lights are back on," I replied.

Mama pulled the curtains open to the living room window. The rain had turned to sprinkles.

When the phone rang, it startled us like we were in an Alfred Hitchcock movie. Sonya and Mary grabbed my arm. I jumped and grabbed Sonya. We laughed and called each other scaredy-cats.

Mike answered the phone. "Mama, it's Aunt Pearl. She's asking about Jeffrey and Sonya."

"No need to worry. They're sitting over here, laughing with the kids," she said. "Okay...Uh-huh."

"I wonder what Aunt Pearl is saying," Sonya said.

"I'll send them home," Mama said. "In a minute, you should see both of them through your kitchen window."

Sonya walked to the door and paused. "Will you guys have to top onions tomorrow?" she asked me.

"I don't know. It depends on the weather."

"Come on, Sonya," Jeffrey said, "before Granddaddy calls for us again."

"Well, I'll see you tomorrow," Sonya crossed her fingers.

I closed the door behind them. I peeked outside and prayed, "God, if it's not too much to ask, could you please bring us more rain tonight? Cousin Sonya just got here."

When I came back into the house, Mike was making peanut butter and jelly sandwiches for our lunches tomorrow. Edward stirred the Kool-Aid. This time he made orange and grape.

Mama hollered from the front bedroom, "Don't drink that Kool-Aid, kids! It's for when we get to the fields tomorrow!"

"Don't worry. I made extra," Edward whispered.

Was this another joke he was playing? I didn't know whether to believe him or not until he showed me. Inside the refrigerator were two more Ball jars of Kool-Aid.

Later that night, I woke up sweating from the heat and heard the refrigerator door close.

Mama was snoring. Maggie had one arm wrapped around Mama, asleep.

I pushed the sheet off and tip-toed out of the bedroom, hesitating when the floor creaked. Not only did I want to go to the bathroom, but I was thirsty and thought about the extra Kool-Aid.

Walking from the bathroom, I saw Thomas close the refrigerator door. The thought in my mind was he probably drank the last of the Kool-Aid.

When I went to grab the extra Kool-Aid, only a little was left.

I pushed back the curtain to the boys' bedroom. "You guys are pathetic," I whispered. "Thomas, why do you always drink the last of the Kool-Aid?"

"What do you mean?" Thomas said.

"You know what I mean. Why make extra when you boys drink the last of anything? I knew it was too good to be true."

"I don't know what you mean," Edward said, flipping his hand in the air.

"What's going on back here?" Mama asked.

"The boys drank the last of the Kool-Aid," I said. "Well, almost the last. They saved two tablespoons."

"I told you kids to stay out of that Kool-Aid."

"Well, Thomas made—"

"It's too early, and we have to get up in a few hours. Now all of you go back to bed."

Chapter 9

I felt someone shaking me. I thought it was part of my dream. Another girl and I were racing inside barrels, trying to see who could roll down a hill the fastest.

"Maggie."

"Huh?" I wiped the sweat from my face. "Mama, it's you?"

"Who else would it be? You need to wake up. Mary can get up in a few minutes."

Mary's leg was sprawled over my waist. I shoved it away.

"Mama, what happened to the fan?" I asked. "Did it break or somethin'?"

"No. It's just hot. I let you sleep a little longer because I wasn't sure of the weather."

Mary and I were in the bathroom washing up when the phone rang. All I heard Mama say was "Okay" and "Uh-huh."

The two of us came inside the bedroom. Mama was sitting on the edge of the bed, humming and reading her Bible.

I didn't know if something bad had happened to someone in the family. After all, that was an early phone call.

"Is everything all right, Mama?" I asked.

"Yes. Why do you ask?"

"Well...you're reading your Bible right after getting that phone call."

"Nothing's wrong. The Holy Spirit told me to read the Scripture, and that's what I did," Mama said. "You and your sister need to get dressed before Uncle Ted honks his horn."

"Didn't it rain enough last night?"

"Most of the rain was on our side of town, away from the field," Mama said.

There was a commotion in the back of the house. Mike was telling Joe to find his shoes and put them on. Edward and Thomas were fussing about who knows what. Mama told them to settle down.

When we walked outside, mist sprinkled against our faces. Uncle Ted was in his red pickup truck, but the lights in his house were still on. He honked the horn. David and Aunt Louise ran past the dining room window and out to their back porch.

Mike and Edward hustled and put our lunches in the back of the station wagon. Mary and I sat in the middle of the front seat and waited for Aunt Pearl, Sonya, and Jeffrey to walk up the footpath.

Mama told us that she had forgotten something inside the house and should be back soon.

It wasn't soon enough for Aunt Louise. She backed her car into our driveway and honked the horn.

Mama got in the car and told me to close the door.

"What about Aunt Pearl and—"

"They're not coming. You can see your cousins when you get home tonight."

I closed the door, slumped down in my seat, and took a bite out of my breakfast sandwich.

Cousin Sonya and Jeffrey had it made. Every summer they took a vacation, slept in, and did whatever they wanted. I had to put on onion-stained jeans every Monday, Wednesday, Friday, and sometimes Saturday.

It didn't matter how much I sulked. Outside of rain, nothing was going to keep us from driving down Rural Route 1 toward White Cloud.

* * *

I was half sleep when I heard the car tires rolling over pebble-filled dirt, causing my head to bounce against the partially opened window.

Tuffy leaped up and down on the car. In between barks, his tongue hung to one side of his mouth.

His day must had been more fun than mine, I thought, chasing after who knows what in the woods, taking naps, and pushing his ball around the yard. At least this time I didn't see porcupine quills stuck around his mouth or smell a skunk on him.

Mike opened his door, and Tuffy ran to greet him, slobbering all over his face. It gave me the opportunity to take the first bath.

I soaked in suds, trying to get the smell of the onion field off me.

"Maggie!" Edward hollered.

I didn't answer.

"Mama, would you please make Maggie get out of the bathroom? The rest of us want to get cleaned up."

"Maggie," Mama said.

"I'm getting out," I said. "But do I have to help Mary?

She just got in the tub."

"Yes, help Mary, but be quick."

There was a knock at the back door. I heard Sonya's voice. Before anyone could say anything, I pulled the bathroom curtain aside and waved for her to come on in.

Mary was bashful and wouldn't get out of the water. No matter how much I promised this or that, she refused.

"That's all right. I'll wait in the living room," Sonya said.

There were many rules in our house. One rule was that no company was allowed in the house when Mama was at work. And in the summer months, when we came home from picking crops, no company was allowed until everyone had cleaned up, eaten dinner, washed dishes, and put leftovers away.

"Mama?" I shuffled my feet around. "Mary cleaned up and I set the table. Can I go outside and sit with Sonya until dinner?"

No answer.

I stood in the doorway, silent, and didn't move.

"Since Sonya is here only for the summer, I'll make an exception. As a matter of fact, ask her if she'd like to stay for dinner."

When I turned around for Sonya, she was standing behind me.

"What are you having for dinner?"

"Beans and cornbread. Do you wanna stay?" I said.

She thought about it first before saying, "Yes."

"You do realize we're havin' beans, right?"

"I probably don't eat beans as much as you do, but our Mama does cook them."

* * *

All summer long, and right on time after picking crops, Sonya waited for me on our back steps. She'd moan and groan about how Aunt Pearl made her clean her room or sweep a floor.

"Well," I'd say, "you can always tell your granddaddy and grandma you'd like to go with us at five in the morning and come home smellin' like onions."

"Hmmm" is all she said, resting her chin on her hands.

"Then, I don't want to hear you whinin'," I said. "Let's play Hopscotch."

Sonya was tall and had long legs. She tossed the rock to the third square. She laughed as she jumped, then tossed it to the tenth and final square. She turned around, hopping on one leg without hesitating or falling over.

I held the rock with sweat dripping down my forehead.

"Take your time, cuz," Jeffrey yelled as he stood behind me.

Sonya moaned so much that I wanted to beat her in the worst way. I swung my arm back and forth and focused on tossing the rock.

"What are you waiting for?" Sonya asked.

I finally tossed the rock and began to jump.

"Maggie," Uncle Ted yelled, "Go get Mike and Edward so they can help me."

My foot landed on the first square. I looked up at Sonya. "That don't count."

"Why not?"

"Because Uncle Ted's shouting made me lose my focus."

Sonya crossed her arms, thinking.

"Maggie!" Uncle Ted hollered. "Did you hear me?"

"Okay," Sonya said. "This time I'll let it slide, but the next time it'll count."

I ran to the house and stopped. Sonya was my cousin and all, but she might cheat. I went back and picked up my rock and put it in my pocket, all the while calling for Mike and Edward.

When they stuck their heads out of the door, I told them that Uncle Ted needed them. After they walked to Uncle Ted's house, I ran back to the game.

I hopped up and down when I saw Mike and Edward carrying big boxes out from Uncle Ted's garage. "Your turn," I told Sonya. I was so curious about what was in the boxes that I missed the hand-off and dropped the rock.

I didn't know if Sonya was cheating or not. I was too distracted by my brothers as they carried one of the boxes.

Mike called Edward an idiot because he couldn't carry a simple box. Edward got mad and dropped the end of the box he was carrying.

"You boys stop all that," Uncle Ted said. "You could lose some of the screws and bolts."

"Here, Maggie!" Sonya said so loudly that I jumped. "Don't you want your turn? What's so important about those boxes anyway? Ever since I've known you, you've always been so nosey."

I couldn't help but watch as Uncle Ted, Mike, and Edward connected the framework of a swing and tightened screws.

"Will you toss the rock?" Sonya said in an angry tone.
"It's a swing set with a slide."
"So what? You act like you've never seen one before."

The swing set probably wasn't that exciting to Sonya because there's a big park next to her family's apartment. Maybe she had forgotten that I live in the country. For me, seeing the swing set was like having Christmas come in the summertime.

I jiggled the rock in my hands, watching Uncle Ted and my brothers assemble the swing set. My desire to be the first one to swing on it grew stronger.

I dropped my rock and ran. I hesitated for a minute to see if Sonya was following me, but she wasn't. She had her hands on her hips.

"Come on," I said. "You know you wanna swing, too."

She had a disappointed look on her face and dropped her rock. She and Jeffrey made eye contact and then raced to the swing set.

"Wait a minute," Uncle Ted said. "It won't be ready tonight. I have to get some other tools to make it safe. Plus, it's dinnertime and I'm hungry. You'll have to wait until the weekend."

"The weekend?" I asked.

"Yep," Edward said. "The weekend. In two days. Sat—"

"I get it."

We watched them carry the swing set, half put together, into the garage. They leaned it against the back wall.

"It's not sturdy enough or ready to leave outside. Plus, I don't want you kids trying to attach the swings." Uncle Ted closed the garage door.

Sonya and I ran to finish our game of Hopscotch. Uncle Ted stopped us, yelling, "Neither of you better bother it or nothing will be put up." He pointed his finger at us and let the screen door slam behind him.

With all of the distractions, Sonya managed to beat me at Hopscotch. I tried to jump onto my space and stumbled. I got up from the ground, wondering how this model-type girl from the city had beat me. I didn't care how long her legs are.

Just as Sonya beat me in hopscotch, Mama called me into the house. Every night at dusk, if my brothers and I were outside, Mama would lean halfway out the door and yell,

"Time to come in."

I told Sonya to toss her rock one more time.

"Did you hear me, Maggie?" Mama hollered. "Don't make me call you again."

"See you tomorrow, Sonya" and I ran into the house.

Shortly after I got in the house, Mama was at the dining room table, braiding Mary's hair. Edward and I argued over who got to the bathroom curtain first.

Mama, as usual, settled any argument. "Maggie, now it seems to me that Edward beat you to the bathroom curtain, so let him wash up first. Don't take long. Everyone has to get up early tomorrow."

"But Mama," I moaned.

"Next time, come inside the first time I call you and you won't have this problem. Make sure to pack extra play clothes for Mary. Mrs. Ollie is going to babysit tomorrow."

Chapter 10

"Whew," Mama said. "It's hot in here. Can you turn the fan on higher?"

"It's as high as it'll go," I said.

With the top of my nightgown, I wiped the sweat from my face while trying to hold the tips of my night rag in the other hand. Afterwards, I wrapped the rag around my head, but I kept losing my grip and had to start over.

Mama saw me struggling and finished wrapping the rag around my braids. Mary's hair was already wrapped.

"Come on, girls," Mama said. "Let's say our prayers. Maggie, it's your turn."

Before going to bed, everyone in the house knelt and said their prayers, always beginning with "Now I lay me down to sleep." Mary stumbled over the words, so after every four words Mary and Mama repeated after me. Once we had prayed, Mama stood at the boy's bedroom door listening to whomever turn it was that night to say their prayers.

Many times I had thought of adding my own words to

the prayer, and sometimes Mama let us. I remembered one time when Mike tried to change the words and whispered a girl's name he wanted to date, thinking Mama didn't hear him. She said out loud, enough that I heard her, "Mike, I don't think that was part of the prayer."

When Mama reached to turn the lamp off, I laid my head on my pillow. Lord, I prayed silently, our family has worked in the fields every summer. Why can't I just play with Sonya more often this summer? Why can't our family take summer vacations? Will you please help? I know that you are probably tired of hearing me complain all the time, but-.

I fell asleep and dreamt that Sonya and I were at Diamond Lake, a small community of summer vacationers and year-rounders west of my family's home. During the summer months, all of the cabins were filled with families from as far away as Ohio and Illinois. Well, at least far away to me.

In my dream, Sonya and I ran in and out of the shallow part of the water. We chased each other on the dock until she jumped off into the deep end.

"Jump!" she yelled.

"You know I can't swim that good," I hollered.

"Jump. I'll catch you."

I backed up to give myself a running start. When I neared the edge of the dock, I changed my mind.

"Chicken!" Sonya swam to me.

We splashed around and got out of the water only to jump back in.

"Maggie, wake up," a voice said.

I began to fall back asleep and was shaken. "Maggie, you have to get up," Mama said.

I moaned and pressed my elbows into the mattress. I rubbed sweat off my face, which I must have thought was the water in my dream.

"Wake your sister up, too. She doesn't need to be completely dressed because I'm going to drop her and Joe off at Mrs. Ollie's house."

She must have baby-sat every child up and down Rural Route 1.

I shook Mary and told her to get up and follow me to the bathroom. All we had to do was to wash the sleep from our eyes.

At the same time, Mama walked through the house and into the kitchen. "Mike," Mama said, "don't forget to pack the gloves for the shears."

The shears were a big, brown, metal, oversized pair of scissors with sharp blades. The gloves protected our hands and fingers from cuts, blisters, and sunburn. They were a necessity for everyone who topped onions.

Last time we forgot our gloves. We rented some from the field chief for five cents a pair. That money was subtracted from our daily payout.

On the way to Mrs. Ollie's house, it was already so hot that Mama told us to roll our windows down. Mama and Mike carried the sleepy twins to Mrs. Ollie's front door and knocked.

When we drove away, I folded my arms on the opened window frame and rested my head against them, staring at Mrs. Ollie's house for as long as I could, wondering, why couldn't I have stayed in my dream?

Mama turned right onto the two-track, snake-shaped road. We drove another mile before the smell of onions became stronger. To shade our car, we parked it as close as we could to the trees.

Multiple families were responsible for one section of an onion field. Today, we were going to work with the Johnsons, Harringtons, Amos, and York family.

Hats in different shapes and colors bobbed up and

down while people topped onions. If we didn't wear hats, we'd probably get sunstroke.

"Everyone, make sure you have your hats and shears," Mama said.

Even with flatbed trucks roaring past, carrying the onion crates to factories, the fields were calm. Every now and then, a family would sing a Christian song, B.B. King, or a "doo whop, doo whop" to break the silence. Once the crates were filled with onions, we'd stack them six high and six wide.

Seven, sometimes six o'clock in the morning, we were already topping with three hours before the first break.

Close to an hour I noticed Mama walking to the car. When she came back, she handed my brothers and me wet rags. Water dripped down the sides of our faces. Many workers did the same, hoping it would keep their heads cooler, but it was short-lived. The sun's rays were too hot.

Johnny, a boy who worked in the fields, tapped my head. I looked up at him from my squatting position, wiping sweat from my forehead.

"Maggie," he said. "You'd better dip your rag before you overheat."

I flipped my hand at him. "I'm not gonna waste a lot of my ice cold water. I can still use it to wipe my face."

"Suit yourself," Johnny said. He walked toward his family's car.

I looked back at him and then turned around and grabbed a handful of onions.

Mama and Aunt Louise were further up in their rows but always kept an eye on us kids, making sure we didn't fall behind too far. Mama had made up a schedule for topping and timed it perfectly so she could know to the penny how much money we'd make for the day.

Thomas and Edward were topping two rows each and

were within ten feet of Mike and me.

    I stood up, wiping the sweat from my face.

    "Maggie?" Mike said. "You all right?"

    "It's just so darn hot out here," I said.

    "Take another water break," Mike said. "I'll keep your rows caught up."

    "That's all right. You're already topping your own rows."

    I knelt back down with no enthusiasm and continued topping row-to-row. The sun was getting hotter.

    I began to daydream, thinking of the beach, and then screamed, dropping my shears and onions.

    "Maggie?" Mama said.

    I tossed my hat off and covered my face with the rag. "Water! Water!" I hollered.

    "Maggie, what happened?" Mama asked. "Did you cut yourself?"

    "No. Some of the onion juice squirted into my eyes."

    "Mike," Mama said in a concerned voice, "you were the closest to her. Hurry and get some water from the car. How did you get the juice in your eyes?"

    "I topped the onions and, next thing I knew, some of the juice squirted."

    "Put your hands down and hold your head back." Mama's voice didn't sound convinced that this had been an accident. She poured the water over my eyes.

    "Louise," Mama said. "Make sure that none of the field chiefs are around."

    "I don't see any of them," Aunt Louise said. "They must be in the other fields."

    We didn't want a field chiefs to know about an injury. If they did, they'd send us home.

    "Hurry, Mike," Mama said. "Get your sister to the car

before we cause more of a scene."

Aunt Louise told the rest of the family to keep working.

My face was covered with sweat, tears, and onion juice. I flinched each time the water was poured onto my face.

"Maggie," Mike said. "Could you tell me again what happened?"

I was crying and sniffling when I told Mike that I used the shears to cut a handful of onions.

"Were you paying attention?" he asked.

I held my head down, tears running down my face.

"Mike," Mama said, "look inside the glove compartment and hand me the bottle of blessed olive oil." She carried a bottle wherever we went and kept one in her purse, coat pocket, and in the glove compartment.

Aunt Louise waved for the rest of the family to gather around the car.

Mama rubbed the blessed olive oil across my eyelid. "In the name of Jesus, heal this child's eye."

I heard quiet "Hallelujahs" from the back of the car to the front. We didn't want to draw too much attention from the other people topping onions.

Mama cuddled with me and wiped the sweat from my forehead. "We might have to go home early today."

Could I be hearing things? I wondered. We only left early if it was raining or lightning.

* * *

I squirmed in the backseat of the car and woke up alone. Even with the windows rolled down, it was still hotter than hell outside.

I opened the door and placed one hand over my bad eye. Mike was walking to the car. "How you doin'?" he asked.

"My eye stings."

He reached to touch it and I flinched. I scooted over to the middle of the backseat and looked in the rearview mirror. I began to lift my hand off my eye but then stopped.

"Go ahead," Mike said. "Look in the mirror. You'll see it's not that bad."

"You wouldn't lie to me, would you?"

"No. To me, it's not so bad."

"I bet it's the size of a golf ball. It sure does feel like one."

"Go on," he said.

I slowly removed my hand. "Mike! It is the size of a golf ball!"

"You'll be fine. But, if I were you, I'd put on some sunglasses before the family comes for lunch."

Mike fiddled around with the passenger side sun visor. Sometimes Mama kept sunglasses there. He looked inside the glove compartment. "What really happened to your eye?"

I sat back in the seat. "Daydreaming—"

"Maggie," Mike said in a disappointed tone.

"I was daydreaming that Sonya and I were outside playing with the hose, and then I topped too close to the onions and squirted myself."

He sighed.

"Please don't tell Mama."

"I won't, but don't you ever do something like that again. You hear? And stop all that daydreamin'."

"Minutes later, I heard Thomas and Edward. I turned around. They were about ten feet away. "Uh-oh."

"Yeah. It's dumb and dumber coming. It must be lunchtime."

Mike reached over the front seat and wiped the tears from my face.

I didn't want Thomas and Edward, of all people, to see me crying. "You won't tell, right?" I asked again.

Mike shook his head and gave me a smile. "I'll keep our little secret...this time. Hurry up and put those sunglasses on."

"This car must be hot as hell," Edward said.

"Stop that cussin'," I said. "Mama taught you better."

"You cuss just as much as I do. And why do you have those sunglasses on? Think you're in Hollywood or something? Everyone knows your eye is swollen."

"Go and sit underneath those shade trees or something," I said. "Better yet, why don't you fall into that ditch over there near the trees?"

Edward and Thomas left. But, soon, other kids sat next to them and looked at our car. One of the boys stood up taking a bite from his sandwich to see if I was inside.

I'd glance out the back window at Edward, Thomas, Lewis and some of the kids sitting under the shade. From their laughter, it seemed like they were having a good time. Edward was probably telling some of his corny jokes that he thought were funny. Thomas poked one of the kids.

"Don't look so sad," Mike said. "At least you're not out in the hot sun topping onions."

I knew he was trying to make me feel better, but I didn't feel like smiling. Maybe it was because of the throbbing pain in my eye or because I knew better than to daydream while topping onions.

"Thanks for the sunglasses, Mike," I said. "I would have never thought of that."

"With the sunhat and sunglasses, you do look like a movie star from Hollywood."

I held my chin up and put one finger on the sunglasses. "Which camera is mine?" I said.

* * *

After lunch Mike moved the car next to the family and rows they were topping. I could hear a lot of the conversations.

"Hey, Charley Louise?" one of the Harringtons said. "How much longer are you and your family topping in this heat today?" They were topping onions next to us.

Mama and Aunt Louise stood up.

"We don't know yet," Mama yelled.

"But not all day," Aunt Louise said.

The two of them walked to the car fanning with their hats. Aunt Louise reached for the water.

"How's your eye?" Mama asked me.

"It's...it's all right. Still hurts and has some throbbing."

"Don't you want to sit outside underneath some shade near the stream?" Mama asked.

"I will," I said. "In a minute."

They walked to the trees near the stream. They probably didn't know that I could still hear most of what they talked about.

"We'll have to top Maggie's rows," Aunt Louise said.

"I know. Mike has been trying to keep them up, but he has his rows too," Mama said. She and Aunt Louise looked back at me.

I quickly turned around so they wouldn't think that I was listening to their conversation.

"We'll have to divide her rows between us," Mama said.

"And take water breaks," Aunt Louise said.

"If we can't finish, the family will be short pay," Mama said.

My brothers walked back to the field, talking with

Lewis. Mama and Aunt Louise's decision didn't sit well with Thomas and Edward. The rest of the family had to work harder and faster in the heat. I felt sorry and sad that everyone topped my rows.

Edward had a handful of onions in his hand. Thomas rested on one of the crates. Lewis was topping, and Mike walked from one row to the other.

Mama walked up to Edward. He dropped the onions he was holding and turned around facing the car. The others followed, Edward walking faster than the rest, stomping his feet.

Edward sat on the back bumper next to Mike and kicked dirt on their break. Everyone else grabbed bottles of water or drank whatever Kool-Aid was left. Lewis went to Aunt Louise's car to drink their water.

"Edward, go and get a drink of water with the rest," Mike said.

I saw Edward's lips move, but I couldn't hear what he whispered.

"Stop being so selfish." Mike stood up in frustration. "Maggie didn't hurt herself on purpose."

"Why can't we just go home and take what we can?" Edward asked.

Before Mike could answer, Mama yelled for the boys, waving her hands.

Everyone but Edward said, "See you later, Maggie."

I rested my chin against the opened car window and watched everyone. The field chief came over to Mama. He looked at his watch and pointed up the rows. I don't know what he said, but everyone began to top faster.

I had fallen asleep and woke up later in the afternoon. By then Mama and Aunt Louise worked the rows alongside Thomas and Lewis. The field chief walked up again. Mike and

Edward had topped the last two rows. Our crates were stacked high on top of each other in between the rows.

Mike and Edward reached for the rags in their pockets and looked for a spot that was clean and dry enough to wipe their sweat. Thomas dragged his feet on the way to the car, making a path in the dirt.

The field chief shook his head, looking up and down the rows in amazement. My hardworking family never left a job undone. He handed Mama and Aunt Louise two white envelopes.

Edward and Thomas glared at me when they got to the car. I thanked them for topping my onions, but it didn't seem to matter.

"How you feeling?" Mama asked. "Let me look at that eye."

"It don't sting as much, but it feels sore and still throbs."

On the car ride home, I leaned my head on the open window, letting the breeze brush against my face. When we neared Mrs. Ollie's house, I asked, "Mama, will I have to top onions tomorrow?"

She didn't answer.

"Mama, did you hear me?"

She turned into Mrs. Ollie's driveway. Joe and Mary sprinted out of the house like there was a fire.

Mary hugged Mama. When she ran over to hug me, she immediately stopped. A tear rolled down her cheek. "What happened to your eye?"

"Don't cry. I'll be all right." I gave her a hug. "The onion juice sprayed into my eye."

"You sure you'll be all right?"

"Yeah. What did you do today?"

Mary and I talked until Mama turned into our driveway.

I again asked Mama, "Will-"

"Maggie, I heard you the first time, honey." She stopped the car. "Let's see how you're feeling later. Okay? Then I'll decide."

"Okay," I mumbled.

I waited for Mike to finish bathing before I ran my bath water. I sunk into the tub and rested my head. I laid a washcloth over my eyes after squeezing out the water.

Chair legs scraped against the dining room floor, and the boys argued.

"Thomas and Edward," Mama yelled. "That can only be the two of you."

They stopped.

"Where are you going in such a hurry?" she asked.

"Outside to clean up with the water hose," Thomas said. "Maggie is taking too long, and we're starvin'."

"Please just clean up. Don't hurt each other by running around."

The washcloth was still over my eyes when a hand touched my shoulder. I flinched, splattering water on the floor.

Mary seemed just as startled as me and bumped into the stool at the other end of the tub. "I was only checking to see how you're feeling. Didn't mean for the water to splash on your eye. Does it hurt worse?"

"It's not any worse than before."

"Mama told me and Joe you weren't feeling good and to not bother you, but—"

"You're not bothering me," I reassured her. "Hand me that towel over there."

Mary reached for the towel. She had more than enough questions for me. "Are you going to lose it?" she asked. "Will you have to get a new one?"

I changed the subject. "How about you help me dry my

back and tell me about your day with Mrs. Ollie."

"Maggie?" Mama asked. "Are you almost done? Mike and I have to clean up so everyone can eat dinner."

After everyone had cleaned up and sat down at the dinner table, I fidgeted in my chair, waiting for Mama to tell me I didn't have to top onions. I gobbled down my mashed potatoes and chicken.

"Maggie," Mama asked, "is there a reason why you're eating so fast? Is there a contest that myself and the rest of the family isn't aware of?"

"Uh-huh," I responded and Mama hadn't made a decision about me working. "Can I be excused from the table?"

"Let's eat as a family. We've had a hard day."

While I sat patiently, the family talked about everything except topping onions.

"Sis, you must be hurting because you didn't want to go out and play with Sonya," Mike said.

"I told her to come over after I wash the dishes." I tapped my spoon on the table until Mama looked at me.

There was an unusual calmness around the table, as though everyone except me knew a secret.

"Everyone should look over the list of chores and check off what has been done," Mama said.

I walked to the refrigerator and rubbed my finger down the list. It took a few minutes for me to adjust my vision. At first, I read the words to myself.

"Anything wrong, sis?" Thomas asked.

I couldn't believe what I was reading. Mama rarely changed the list. But, to my surprise, Thomas was going to clean the table and wash the dishes.

"Thomas, is this a joke? Are you really going to do my chores tonight?"

"Well, sis," he said. "I'm not a complete meanie.

I know you didn't squirt that onion juice in your eyes on purpose. That must have hurt really badly."

I sat in the living room in shock. For once, I didn't hear Thomas complain.

By night time, Mama hadn't made a decision, and I didn't want to be a pest. I tossed and turned throughout the night.

The next morning, I looked through a gap in the curtain. There was sunlight. Mama was asleep. Except for the boys snoring loudly, the rest of the house was quiet.

"Mama," I said anxiously. "Mama."

"What, child?" she responded in a groggy tone.

"Aren't we going...?"

She had a weird smile on her face, as if there was another secret no one told me.

"Calm down," Mama said. "I wanted to surprise you."

"What surprise?" I asked.

"There will be no topping onions today."

At first, I was so surprised that I couldn't move. My feet seemed to be glued to the floor. Then I jumped up and down and ran to wake my brothers.

I flung the bedroom curtain aside and bumped into them in the living room. "You knew about it?" I asked.

"Everyone sit down," Mama said. "As we all know, Maggie had an accident yesterday at the onion field. Because she needs to begin the healing process, so, today we won't be topping any onions."

My brothers and I expressed our excitement with "Oh, yeah" and "Thank you, Jesus."

"Maggie, I'll take you to Doc Douglas in town and let him look at that eye," Mama said. "He'll tell me when you can top onions. Before the doctor appointment, the laundry needs to be sorted through and folded. The rest of the family will help with the chores, and I'll add to your list of chores as need be."

Since the boys were completing my chores, it was my responsibility to watch the twins, which meant watching cartoons. I hated cartoons, except for the Road Runner. The twins loved Popeye. I watched and tried my hardest to stay awake.

The screen door slammed. "What's happening, everyone?" Sonya asked. "Oh my God," she said when she saw me. "Did the onions punch you in the face?"

"Ha ha," I said.

"I heard what happened. I guess you don't want to finish our game of Hopscotch, huh?"

"Boy, news sure does travel fast. How did you find out?"

"Aunt Pearl and Aunt Louise were talking on the phone. I overheard how everyone prayed over your eye in the car and topped your rows."

"This family has to tell everything," I said. "Sometimes that bothers me."

"You should be happy they care so much. When will the doctor see you?"

"They talked about that too?"

"Yeah."

Sonya and I wanted to go outside, so somehow I had to convince Thomas to watch Joe. Mary would follow me and Sonya.

Thomas was in the bedroom reading his comic books. I quietly pushed the curtain back and walked up to his bed with one hand over my eye. "Thomas, Sonya and I want to go outside, but Joe is watching cartoons. Would you watch him for me?" I tried to look pitiful to make him feel sorry for me.

Sonya clasped her hands together and said, "Please? Please?"

"Okay," he said. "But only because of your eye."

When we got outside, Mama was hanging clothes on the clothesline. "Who's watching Joe?"

"Thomas said he'd watch him for me."

A concerned look spread over Mama's face. Thomas wasn't the best baby-sitter. Mama also didn't want me to abuse a privilege by trading off a responsibility. "Okay. This time," she said.

Noise came from inside Uncle Ted's garage. We didn't see anyone at first. Uncle Ted dragged a box underneath the big oak tree near his house. Mike and Edward carried another box.

Uncle Ted told the boys, "Wait for Uncle John to help before you open the boxes or you might drop some of the screws." The screws were for the swing set that Uncle Ted had begun to build.

"How many screws do you think the boys will lose?" I asked Sonya.

"Most of them," I said.

We giggled.

Mike and Edward dropped one of the swing arms. The screws fell to the ground.

"You boys are hardheaded," Uncle Ted said. "I told you to wait for your Uncle John."

As soon as those words left his mouth, Uncle John walked up the footpath between our houses. Jeffrey ran ahead of him. "Keep up, Grandpa," he said.

Uncle John grunted.

Aunt Louise leaned out the screen door of her house and asked about the commotion. When she saw the swing set being built and nobody fighting, she rested against the car to watch.

The swing set wasn't a big deal to Sonya and Jeffrey, but to us, it was more thrilling than sitting on the steps playing a game of "Who can toss a rock the furthest?" or "Whose pig can grunt the most?"

When Uncle Ted asked for someone to sit in the swings, I leaped up, one hand over my eye. They wanted to make sure the screws, bolts, and nuts were secure.

"Okay. You can get up," he said. "Now all we have to do is let the cement dry. It'll have to dry before anyone can swing."

"How long will that take?" I asked.

"Oh." Uncle Ted lifted his cap and scratched the top of his head. "Probably a few days."

"Shoot." I stomped the ground.

"Just have patience," Sonya said. "It's only a swing."

"Maggie," Mama hollered, "you can't swing until the doctor sees you about your eye anyway."

Doc Nelson examined my eye. He told Mama to have me wait a week before topping any more onions.

During the week I didn't top onions, Mary, Sonya and I grew closer. We played a game of how many trucks and cars drove up and down the road. She counted the cars and I counted the trucks. Mary was the deciding win. Behind our house, near Mama's vegetable garden, we made a big house between the trees. Every now and then Sonya reminded me of my eye, to be careful that no dirt got in it.

"For a girl from the city, you make a good leaf house," I said.

Sonya didn't smiled.

The following week at super, Mama made an announcement.

"Well, Doc Douglas says that Maggie's eye is healing.

At least good enough to go back to the fields. So, next week, we'll be returning."

The week off went by faster than any of us wanted, but I think no more than for Mary. That night at super, I noticed sadness on Mary's face.

"In the morning, Mrs. Ollie will continue to watch you and Joe," Mama said to the twins.

It was a relief that Mrs. Ollie watched the twins. Otherwise they'd have to sit in the hot car.

That night Mary helped me clean the table. I couldn't shut her up. "Maggie," she said, "are you listening to me?"

"Yes." I prayed silently that she didn't ask me to repeat what she had asked because I really wasn't listening.

A cool breeze brushed against us while we sat on the back steps. I perked up when I saw Sonya skipping on the footpath.

The swing set was finally ready to use. Sonya and I swung into the night, laughing and competing to see who could touch the highest leaf on the tree. Then the swing set nudged forward.

We came to a stop, scared that it might tip over. We sat in the swings, making circles in the sand with our feet, not talking until Sonya asked me, "What's it like cutting up onions and picking cherries every summer?"

"Well, first of all, you don't cut them, you top them with big shears."

Sonya had a confused look on her face.

I pulled a handful of grass from the ground. "Pretend there is a ball at the bottom of this grass. Think of my fingers as scissors. Do you understand now?"

"Sorta."

"Believe me, you never wanna do it."

"You're probably right."

"Do you wanna swing high again?" I asked.

"I think we'd better wait until Uncle Ted has a chance to make sure the swing is secure."

Then, with a quick push of her feet, Sonya acted like she was going to swing but stopped quickly. "I tricked you. I wasn't going swing."

Jeffrey stopped in front of the swings, slipping in the sand.

"That was dangerous, Jeffrey," I said. "What if we were swinging? That would had been a bad accident."

"Yeah," Sonya said. "Maybe hitting some sense into that big noggin you call a head would help."

"Did Uncle Ted say that anyone could swing?" he asked. "If so, seems like you two have been in it long enough. Let someone else have a turn."

"You can be a real pain in the—" Sonya said.

"Uncle Ted needs to make sure the swing set is secure first," I said. "It was wobbling."

"And don't you dare cuss, Sonya," Jeffrey said, "or I'll tell Grandpa."

Chapter 11

On Tuesday and Thursday, at ten o'clock in the morning, without fail, our back door opened and slammed.

"Good morning, Sonya," Mike and Thomas yelled from their bedroom.

"Can't you knock?" Edward asked. "I know people must knock in Chicago."

Sonya didn't answer. Instead, she ran into my bedroom and hopped onto the bed. "You haven't finished putting on your clothes yet?"

"This is Tuesday, our day off," I said. "I can have a day of rest, can't I?"

Sonya was wearing a white, short-sleeved, polka-dotted blouse and white shorts that stopped at the middle of her thighs. "Pretty blouse," I said, fumbling through my dresser drawer. Not that I was going to find any clothes that were the same. Hers all came from city stores.

"Thank you," Sonya said. "Mama bought us some new clothes for the summer..." She hesitated.

She had brought four suitcases from Chicago: a large one for her bulky and heavier clothes, in case it got cold; two mid-size suitcases that carried her shorts, blouses, panties, socks, and things like that; and one small suitcase for her hair combs, brushes, curlers, barrettes, lotion, hair grease, and four different colored night rags.

There was no way I could compete with her store-bought wardrobe. I put on my handmade blue shorts with elastic in the waist, white socks, and a short-sleeve white blouse.

"Beat you to the chair," Sonya said. She ran before giving me a chance to lace my sneakers.

"Cheater!" I yelled. I plopped onto her lap.

"How did this chair get out here? Your mama didn't want to throw it away?" Sonya asked.

"Mama was going to have Mike and Edward toss it in the back woods but put it on the front porch instead."

The stuffing hung from both arms. On the right side, one of the legs had broken off. A spring near the back of the seat was starting to rip through the cushion.

Sonya and I didn't care. We put a brick underneath the broken leg. Mama didn't want the spring to poke us, so she had made a large pillow for the seat.

The days our family didn't top onions, Sonya and I raced to the front porch to that oversized chair. Whoever reached it first chose which side of the chair to sit on. Sonya sat on her favorite side near the road and I sat on the other side.

"Let's plan our summer vacation," Sonya said.

"You mean your summer vacation."

"Just get a piece of paper, Maggie."

Mama's notebook was sitting on the dresser. I ripped a piece of paper out, but not before seeing an envelope addressed to Daddy.

I touched the letter three times, tempted to open it. The better part of me said not to, but the curious side of me wanted to.

Slowly, I lifted the unsealed flap and unfolded the letter. The part that caught my eyes was Mama asking Daddy for money, writing that my brothers and I needed clothes, shoes, and food and that the roof needed to be fixed.

"Maggie, where you at?" Sonya asked.

"I'll be right there." As carefully as I could, I refolded the letter where the seams were, put it back inside the envelope, and closed the notebook.

I sat down next to Sonya.

"What took you so long?" she asked.

I didn't answer. Reading that letter put me in an unhappy place.

"Maggie?" Sonya nudged me. "Are you all right?"

I still didn't answer, thinking about the letter.

"Maggie!" Sonya said again.

"I'm sorry. Had problems finding the notebook paper."

Sonya said, "How about we write a list of all the things we want to do this summer and cross them out as we go along?"

"That sounds good."

"We can call it 'our secret list'. It will be something the boys don't know about." Sonya smiled.

To me, there was nothing secret about a list of things to do for the summer. Heck, Mama made lists for everything and didn't keep them a secret. But, since Sonya was here only for the summer, I decided to go along with calling it "our secret list."

"Okay," I said, "but you know Sunday is the Lord's Day, and our family never does anything on Sunday except go to church and pray. We can't even watch television."

"All day in church?" Sonya asked. Wrinkles formed in her forehead and nose.

"Yep, no different than last summer."

"Then Monday it is."

"What should go on the list? Hmmm."

"Hmmm," Sonya repeated. "What should go on the list?"

I tapped the pencil eraser against my forehead. "How about swinging, racing, writing in our diaries...Wait a minute, I made a mistake."

A loud noise came from across the road in the field where the boys were playing baseball. Sonya turned around. "Oh look, your brother just hit a pop fly."

"Sonya," I said.

"He's still running." Sonya went to stand on the top step of the porch with the twins. "Run faster, Mike!"

"Pay attention, Sonya."

She told me something else to put on the list, and again I messed up. This time the paper ripped.

"Let me write it." Sonya grabbed the pencil and paper out of my hands. "I can write faster and neater anyway."

We added to our list to write letters to our cousins Lee and Dave, who lived in Chicago around the block from Sonya and Jeffrey.

"Are Lee and Dave really gonna visit next summer?" I asked.

Sonya shrugged her shoulders.

Lee and Dave were the same age as us and loved baseball. They had only visited White Cloud once.

Sonya added Hopscotch and board games to the list. The sound of tires rolling on gravel distracted us. When we looked up, no cars had passed by the house.

Sonya stopped writing. I leaned against the chair and

saw a car turn into our driveway.

We ran to the bathroom window. There were two carloads of church choir members.

"Can I stay and listen to the choir practice?"

"I don't think Mama will mind," I said. "Let's ask."

Mama was outside and had finished hanging up a small load of clothes on the clothesline that she had washed. By mistake, I had left the secret list on the dining room table. I ran back inside the house. Sonya waved the list at me. She smiled and shook her head.

Mama walked through the door behind me. I jumped.

"You all right, Maggie?" Mama asked.

"Yes, ma'am. Everything is fine. Mama, can Sonya stay for choir practice?"

"I don't see why not. Maybe Sonya would like to join the choir, just for the summer?"

Sonya shied away and sat on the couch.

The practice lasted for one and a half hours. I was surprised that Sonya stayed the entire time. Maybe she would change her mind about joining.

Uncle John seldom let Sonya and Jeffrey stay after dusk. I began to wonder why she wasn't going home and if something was wrong.

The last choir member walked out of the door. "See you Sunday."

Mama closed the piano cover. "If the Lord says the same."

"Do you want to sit on the front porch?" Sonya asked.

Mama interrupted before I answered. "Maggie, go into the bathroom and get the hair grease. I need to comb Mary's hair for church tomorrow."

Sonya was behind me, waiting for an answer. "You know Uncle John's gonna call for you if you're not home soon," I said.

"Maybe he'll let me spend the night."

"You must be joking, right?"

"Ah, yeah, you're probably right."

We sat on the front porch for ten minutes and then heard voices. The Harris boys pressed their bodies against the corner of our house, peeking around it.

I tapped on the window. "What are you guys doing?"

"Shhh." They gestured for us to be quiet.

"What'll you give me if I don't yell out your hiding place?"

"Don't you dare, or the next time I'll tell yours."

"Forget about them," Sonya said. "Do you want play a game of tic-tac-toe?"

When we were playing the second game, I noticed she wasn't paying close attention to where she wrote her mark. "Sonya," I said, "are you sure you wanna put your X there?"

"Oh, I'm sorry. I meant to mark here."

I put my pencil inside a square to draw a circle. Sonya touched my hand. She had a concerned look, as if she had done something wrong or gotten into trouble. "Can you keep another secret?"

I completed the circle to win the game. "What's wrong with you and these darn secrets?"

Sonya balled the paper and tossed it beside the chair. She stared across the road.

"And who am I keeping this secret from? You don't know anybody."

She crossed her arms. "Can you?"

"Okay. Okay."

"Last night, I heard something outside my window. Maybe a bear."

"A bear?" I tried my hardest not to laugh. "What gave

you that cockamamie idea?"

"The past two weeks I've slept with the lights on. There's something rustling around in the bushes outside my bedroom window."

I burst out laughing.

Sonya gave me a dirty look. Her eyes grew bigger and bigger as she described what she thought was a bear and how it wasn't funny.

"It was probably Tuffy or the neighbor dog. What do you know about bears besides what you read in your school books? Do you have any in Chicago?"

No matter how much I tried to convince her we didn't have bears lurking around our houses, she wouldn't believe me. She held my arm. "Will you spend the night?"

"That's the big secret?"

Sonya didn't answer and just sat there staring at me.

"I'll have to ask Mama. Right now she's at Aunt Louise's house. And no, I won't call her. She'll be home soon enough."

We sat on the front porch and watched Mike, Edward, and the neighbors play hide-n-seek. When we heard the back door shut, both of us leaped from the chair and ran into the dining room.

"Does your granddaddy know you're here?" Mama asked Sonya.

Sonya and I talked over each other. Mama's eyes moved back and forth from Sonya to me, not knowing who to listen to. "Slow down. One at a time."

"Mama, I know it's Saturday, but can I spend the night with Sonya?"

Before Mama answered, the phone rang. Mama said, "I'll send her home right away." She went to hang up the phone and stopped. "Oh, John, let me speak to Pearl." Mama looked at me and Sonya. "Pearl, Maggie wants to spend the night with Sonya. Is that all right?"

When Mama hung up the phone, she said, "You can spend the night, but you have to be home in the morning to try on your church dress."

"Wait," I told Sonya. "I need to grab some pajamas."

"You can sleep in a pair of mine."

We hurried through the dining room, bumping into the chairs. Before Mama could tell us not to slam the door or run in the house, we were outside.

The Harris boys were hiding in a different spot. Sonya and I looked at each other. At the same time, we yelled, "Oh, by the way the Harris boys are hiding behind the tree next to Tuffy's doghouse." We giggled and raced to Uncle John's house. Sonya beat me, but only because I couldn't see out of my eye.

When we reached the doorstep, Sonya said, "The city girl finally won."

I smiled. "Wait until my eye heals."

We rushed past Aunt Pearl, who was in the kitchen. "Why is it that you kids have to run and slam doors every time you go in or out?"

"I swear girl, everyone tells us that," I said.

"What?"

"To stop slamming doors and running through the house."

Aunt Pearl opened the door to the bedroom to remind us that church was in the morning and to not stay up late. When she left, I asked Sonya to show me where she thought the bear sound was coming from.

Sonya took baby steps to the window and stopped. She pointed to the bushes.

I asked her to stand aside and opened the window. By

the time I turned around, Sonya was standing near the wall, close to her bed.

"Sonya, stop acting silly."

After lowering the window, I looked into her eyes. "Sonya, I've lived here all my life and have never seen a bear on our land."

Sonya walked away with her shoulders slumped. She seemed disappointed that I didn't believe her.

She sat on the chair in front of Aunt Pearl's vanity and opened the drawer where she kept her hair rollers and hair rags.

The vanity had three mirrors: one in the middle, and one on each side that folded. Sonya turned one of the mirrors outward and handed me a roller. "Maggie, will you help roll my hair? And cuz, make sure my ends—"

"I've been rolling Mama and Mary's hair since the third grade, although most of the time we wore braids or ponytails." I gave Sonya a sharp eye.

Sometimes a mirror can be great for extended conversation. Sonya didn't say another word.

"Sonya, I'm sorry. I'll make sure your hair is rolled the right way."

I rolled the ends straight and flattened them against the thin paper that was cut into a small square to fit the roller. Otherwise, by morning time, the ends would be bushy.

I had already put four big rollers into Sonya's hair when she went to hand me another one. I paused. Our eyes met in the mirror.

"Are you all right?" Sonya asked.

"Chicago...it's a real big city?"

"Are you kidding? There are so many cars on the streets bumper-to-bumper. The apartment buildings are five, six, or seven stories high, close to each other, almost connecting, and separated by alleys." The more Sonya described Chicago, the more her excitement grew. I could tell she missed being home with her family and friends.

I half-smiled as I listened to her talk about Chicago. I finished rolling one section of her hair and turned her head sideways to do the other. "Have you seen my daddy?" I asked. "Do you know he lives in Chicago?"

Sonya moved, but we didn't make eye contact in the mirror.

"He lives on Morgan Street, the south side," I said. "Do you live near him?"

Her face turned from excitement to sadness. "I live on the east side of Chicago," Sonya said. "The only time I'd even heard your daddy's name was when my grandparents talked to your mama."

Sonya waited before handing me the last roller. She looked at me as if she wanted to say something else, but she didn't.

I continued to brush her hair. Then she reached over her shoulder and touched my hand. "How did Granddaddy and the rest of the family find White Cloud? It's so far away from civilization."

"I answered this same question for you last year," I said. "Do you think I left something out?"

"You must have because the story is too good to be true."

Chapter 12

After rolling the last section of Sonya's hair, I took a deep breath and sat on the end of the bed. Sonya turned halfway and rested her chin on the back of the chair.

"Well, Mama told us that Grandma worked as a housekeeper in Chicago," I said. "Grandma began to grow tired of the city. She didn't feel it was right for Mama, who was a teenager at the time, to continue to grow up around pimps and prostitutes."

Sonya didn't say a word. She just stared as if I was reading from one of Uncle John's books.

I scooted on the bed until my back rested against the wall. "Grandma was sitting at a bus stop in Chicago when a man by the name of Mr. Little talked to her about land in Michigan. It was affordable and a great place for coloreds to live and raise a family."

"You have got to be making this up," Sonya said.

"No. This is a true story. Do you want me to continue?"

Sonya nodded.

"Mr. Little came to the house in Chicago for dinner and met the rest of the family. He showed them pictures of other coloreds who lived in a town called Baldwin, Michigan."

"Not White Cloud?" Sonya asked.

"Sonya," I said. "I've told you this story before and I'm tired of repeating it. Just accept it. We live in a small town with dirt roads. Can we leave it at that?"

Sonya shoved the chair away from the vanity, came and sat next to me, and put her arms around my shoulders. "Maybe Cousin Charley Louise, I mean your mama, will let you visit me in Chicago, and then we can find your daddy." Sonya smiled.

"Maybe."

A knock on the door startled us. Aunt Pearl peeked inside. "It's time for bed."

"Reach underneath the bed for the flashlight," Sonya told me. "That's where I keep my diary."

The two of us laid underneath the sheet. We read and giggled at some of her diary entries. On one page, Sonya had written how she had passed to the sixth grade, and her mama almost didn't let Jeffrey pass to the fourth grade because of his grades.

"What! Your mama was going to flunk him?"

We heard a knock on the wall. Startled, Sonya hid further underneath the sheet. Uncle John and Aunt Pearl's room was right next to ours. Their house was large, but the walls must have had paper for insulation. "Girls!" Aunt Pearl said.

"What are you flinching for?" I whispered to Sonya. "It's just Aunt Pearl."

Sonya turned the flashlight off, mad because I teased her. "Wait until tonight. We'll see who gets the last laugh."

***

In the late afternoon, Uncle Ted knocked on the back door and told my brothers and sister, "I have a swimming pool in my backyard. You can come and test it out."

When I got to Uncle Ted's, someone pushed my shoulder, telling me to jump in. I brushed his hand away and focused on the water that rippled from the warm breeze. He pushed my shoulder again to what I thought was the water, but instead it wasn't a splash, I hit the floor. I squinted and looked around.

"Maggie, wake up."

I wiped the sleep from my eyes and turned around to face Sonya. "There's no pool?"

Sonya didn't know how upset I was at her for waking me up only to tell me that I was dreaming.

"There's noise outside the window." Sonya grabbed onto my arm, squeezing it.

The room was dark. "The only thing I hear is that old fan in the corner."

"You must hear that noise. Go look out the window."

I stumbled over a house shoe and almost fell at the window. "Sonya, I don't see anything. Maybe you can help me."

"No way."

"Stop being a scaredy-cat."

Sonya tiptoed to me and stopped. "You can't hear that noise?"

"No. As a matter of fact, the only thing scaring me is you."

I pulled the curtains aside. At first, we couldn't make out anything.

"Here, use the flashlight," Sonya said.

I smiled to myself, wondering if I should tell her.

"What is it?"

"Well...I'm not sure. Maybe you're right."

"See, I told you."

I thought, how much longer should I keep her in suspense? "You know, you could be right, but it would be awfully hard for the Harris' dog, Sparky, to eat you."

"What? A dog?"

"That darn dog always gets out at night and roams the yards."

We watched Sparky rustle through the bushes and chew on a bone.

"Have you been tossing food out the window?" I asked.

"Only a few chicken bones here and there."

"You better be careful tossing food out your window, or one night something else might show up."

A door closed. "Hurry," I said. "Get back in bed."

Sonya jumped in the bed first and snuggled up against the wall, pretended to be asleep. "It wasn't grandma," she whispered. "She would have peeked in the room."

"Maybe it was Jeffrey," I said.

"I don't know. Let's get back in bed."

* * *

Sonya and I woke up to the smell of bacon, toast, scrambled eggs, and pancakes.

"You girls better get up if you want to eat before church," Aunt Pearl hollered.

When Sonya and I went into the dining room and pulled the chairs out from the table, Aunt Pearl said, "Go into the bathroom and wash your face and hands. And Maggie, don't forget your mama has to finish hemming your skirt."

It was different eating at Aunt Pearl's house compared to mine. Uncle John sat at one end of the table and Aunt Pearl at the other. The kids always sat in the middle on either side. The food was passed around in a civilized manner with no fussing or fighting.

I sat in the chair that I did at home. I wished our table at home had both a Mama and Daddy at it, but I knew that Daddy wasn't coming back.

"Ouch," I said. Jeffrey had kicked my leg. I stretched to rub it and frowned at him. He ignored me, eating his scrambled eggs.

Uncle John looked up from his food. Before he could say a word, I pointed at Jeffrey and frowned. Uncle John didn't give Jeffrey the usual stare-down. In a deep voice, he called Jeffrey's name. That was it.

Jeffrey, Sonya and I looked at Aunt Pearl. She gestured as if to say, "Let it go."

It wasn't fair. Jeffrey made eye contact with me and smiled. I waited a second or two and smiled back.

Uncle John placed his fork and knife on his plate. He looked at Sonya, Jeffrey, and then me. "I see you have plenty of time to harass each other. Tell me about the books I gave you to read for summer break. How are you coming along with them?"

"I read the first book," Sonya said. She loved to read, romance books mostly.

Uncle John looked at Jeffrey. He swallowed his glass of milk, trying to prolong the inevitable. "I read half a book."

Uncle John picked up his fork. "You've read only half a book but have been here over a month? How many pages is that a day?"

Jeffrey sunk in his chair. "I don't know."

"Maggie, how about you?"

"Well..."

Aunt Pearl got up to answer the phone. "Uh-huh...yes, I'll send her home right away." She came back to the table. "Maggie, your mama told me that you need to come home. I can wrap up your breakfast."

"Let me help you, Aunt Pearl," I said.

A few minutes later, I left.

Uncle John said, "Don't forget about the books."

"Okay."

I hadn't read one book this summer. Uncle John was big on reading. Every Christmas, he gave us a book for a present, and every summer, we had to read at least one book and give him a verbal report. I'm quite sure he thought reading books would inspire us, but who reads during the summer? It's bad enough picking crops.

* * *

Mama hemmed my Sunday go to church dress and asked me to try it on. "Okay, it looks fine. You can finish getting dressed. We're late."

Mary and I sat in the living room while my brothers bumped into each other going from their bedroom to the bathroom.

"Come on," Mama said. "Uncle John and Aunt Pearl are parked on the side of the road next to the driveway."

"Mama I'm in the bathroom and I can see Uncle Ted and Aunt Louise sitting in their car. He just honked his horn," Mike said.

Like every Sunday morning, all three families followed each other down Rural Route 1.

When we drove into the church parking lot, there was a car parked to the right of the church doors. Three boys were chasing each other around the car. Two girls leaned against the car, their eyes focused on us. A man was fanning himself with a straw hat, and the woman next to him had a fan.

Uncle Ted stepped out of his car. As the man walked to him, he reached his hand out. "My name is Mr. Wilson." He turned back to his family. "We live up the road around the bin there."

"Nice to meet you," Uncle Ted said.

After the Wilson boys got out of the car, they shook my brothers, Jeffrey and Lewis' hand. But, the girls, we stood outside of our cars staring at each other.

I took a deep breath. "Hi, my name is Maggie. This is my sister, Mary, and this is my cousin, Sonya."

There was an awkward silence.

"So, you're new to White Cloud, huh?" I asked.

"Yeah. My name is Lisa and this is my sister, Laura."

"Nice to meet you," I said.

Uncle Ted opened the church doors. We walked in, fanning ourselves. The Wilsons followed us. They looked left to right and whispered to each other.

"John and I have to open the rest of the church," Uncle Ted said. "Do you mind opening the windows so that the devil's heat can fly on out of here?" Uncle Ted smiled.

The Wilson boys chuckled. Their parents smiled and opened the windows on each side of the church.

Extra Bibles were kept inside Pastor Johnson's office. I went into his office, brought out an armful of Bibles, and handed them to Mary, Sonya, and the Wilson girls. Most of the congregation brought their own Bibles. Pastor Johnson wanted every person who attended service to read Scripture. Bibles were placed on the last seat on each side of the aisle. The ushers handed them out.

The church wasn't full. The choir marched down the

center aisle to the choir stand. I waved at Sonya, who sat in the second row next to Aunt Pearl.

After praying, Pastor Johnson asked all visitors to stand. The Wilsons hesitated. I think they were shy. Mama made eye contact with Mrs. Wilson, who whispered in her husband's ear.

I noticed that Uncle Ted made eye contact with Mr. Wilson too. "Pastor Johnson," Uncle Ted said. "I'd like to introduce the Wilson family. They graciously helped me and Deacon Glover prepare the church for services this morning. They were the first ones to arrive at church."

Mrs. Wilson smiled at her husband and touched his shoulder.

"Thank you, Mr. Wilson, for your help," Pastor Johnson said. "The Lord likes a willing worker. Please stand and introduce your family."

Mr. Wilson smiled and stood. He introduced his family one at a time, beginning with his wife.

The church sang the welcome song, hugged the Wilson's, and shook their hands.

Pastor Johnson turned to face the choir. "Let's clap for our choir," he said. "I know that Sister Dorsey works hard getting everyone prepared for Sunday. What will the choir sing today?"

"The choir will sing only one song today," Mama said. "We want to honor the pastor's time."

The church members knew Pastor Johnson had to speak at a church in Muskegon this afternoon, but the visitors didn't. Some looked disappointed that the service would be cut short. Sonya didn't. The only time she and Jeffrey went to church was when they were visiting their granddaddy.

Pastor Johnson's speaking engagement at another church meant that Sonya and I would have plenty of time to play and sit on the front porch.

When church services were over, Mama called my brothers and sister to a corner of the church. "As I told you earlier today me, Uncle Ted and Aunt Louise will travel to listen to Pastor Johnson in Muskegon," Mama said. "Listen Edward and stop looking out the window. Okay, Mike is in charge and you are <u>all,</u> including you Thomas, to listen to him, okay?" We nodded. "You will eat at Uncle John's house. Our portion of the food that we will share with theirs is sitting on our kitchen counter top and <u>all</u> of you are to help Mike carry it over to their house. Is that understood?" We nodded again. "Since we have to drive by our house to get to Muskegon, I'll be able to drop you off home. Remember, you behave while I'm away this afternoon."

Pastor Johnson called the church members outside in the church parking lot, making sure who was and was not driving in the caravan too Muskegon. When Mama got to our house the cars pulled off to the side of the road. Mama parked in our driveway and rode with Aunt Louise and Uncle Ted.

I changed from my church clothes and went into the kitchen. That's when I overheard Edward and Mike.

"Why you always gotta be the boss of us?" Edward said. "I'm almost as old as you."

"Come on Edward," Mike said. "I didn't ask to be nobody's boss. Just change your clothes and help get the food to Uncle John's house."

Edward walked from the bedroom flipping the curtain to their doorway. He wasn't happy with Mama's decision to put Mike in charge.

It was five p.m. when we finished dinner and cleaned the table. Aunt Pearl helped my brothers and I pack our leftovers to take home.

At first we left slowly. Mike held the pan of macaroni

and cheese in both hands and Edward the cornbread.

"I bet I'll beat you Edward, Mike said."

And off they went.

"You better not drop that food!" I yelled.

"Just don't forget to feed Tuffy," Mike yelled back to me.

Before I got to Tuffy he was already riled up from Mike and Edward running.

I kneeled down and fluffed his matted, dingy white hair. "I guess you have to eat, too, don't you? I'll be right back."

Soon afterwards, I scraped the leftover bones and scraps from our dinner into his pan. Tuffy began eating as if he hadn't eaten all day.

"Maggie."

I heard a voice and looked up. It was Sonya skipping down the footpath.

Mama had given the boys permission to play baseball across the road with the Harris' while she was gone. The twins watched the game from the front porch steps but weren't allowed to go across the road. Every time Mike, Thomas, or Edward struck someone out or caught a fly ball, the twins cheered.

Sonya and I sat on the front porch, squeezed together in the oversized chair. "Look at those two jumping up and down like they're at a real baseball game," Sonya said, nodding at the twins.

"To them, they are at a real baseball game," I said. "Or at least this is the closest they'll ever probably get to one."

"You mean you have never gone to a real baseball game?"

I hung my head down and flipped the pages in my diary. "No," I said. "Every summer our family picks crops."

"Oh."

"I suppose you've gone to plenty of games, huh?"

"Jeffrey, me, Cousin Ralph, and Jerry have," Sonya said. "We've seen the Chicago White Sox plenty of times. Ralph carries his baseball glove to all of the games, hoping to catch a home run ball, foul ball, or fly ball. Maybe you can visit us in Chicago and go to a game."

"Maybe. For now, let's read our diaries."

We switched diaries. Sonya had the most interesting stories. I read one about a pimp who always parked his white Cadillac on the corner, fighting with his hoes. I gasped. "Wow, Sonya. You won't find anything in my diary like yours."

In my diary, I wrote about the pigs, topping onions, picking cherries, and Edward and Cousin William finding snakes in the backwoods. Mama went to wash the clothes, and a handful of snakes dropped out of Edward's overall pockets. Mama screamed, ran inside the house, and grabbed Edward by his shirt collar. She made him rake near the edge of the garden until dusk.

Sonya and I laughed until tears rolled down our faces.

"Did Edward bring any more snakes into the house?" Sonya asked.

"He didn't dare. His next punishment might have been tougher than the last one."

Sonya's face turned serious. She said that she wanted to tell me something, but she was interrupted when one of the Harris boys hit a home run. The twins jumped up and down. Sonya hurried out the screen door and jumped with them, just as if they were at a real game.

If I had had a camera, I would have taken a picture. Instead, I sat in the oversized chair by myself, wondering what Sonya had wanted to say.

Sonya came back inside. We wiggled to the back of the oversized chair.

"That was real nice of you," I said.

"What do you mean?"

"The twins won't forget it. You made them feel like they were at a real game."

"Where did those dark clouds come from?"

"Looks like rain," I said. "Sometimes it will be light outside and then, suddenly, dark clouds roll in."

"Maggie." Sonya held her head down. "I don't know if I want to come back next summer."

"What!" I said. "Why not?"

"I'm not a country girl like..." Sonya stopped. She looked up at me.

"You mean like me?"

"I don't mean it like that," Sonya said. "But you're used to living here."

As Sonya continued to talk, her voice became distant. I was listening but didn't want to listen.

"Maggie," Sonya said. "Are you listening to me?"

I continued to be silent.

"Maggie, it's not just the city life that I miss. Everything smells up here. It stinks, and I miss the noise of Chicago."

"But Sonya." A tear began to roll down my cheek. "I don't want to lose our summer days of laughing, playing house in the woods, swinging, sitting on the front porch, counting the cars and trucks, and playing whatever games we make up."

"You'll have memories," Sonya said.

I stood up and leaned against the wall, facing the chair. Sonya sat back even further into the seam of the chair.

"But won't you miss anything? What about the conversations we've had on this front porch in this chair? Won't you miss having those?"

"Maggie, please sit down." Sonya stood up and said in

a sad voice, "There's something else I need to tell you. Daddy called last night."

"Please don't tell me he's cutting your vacation short."

Sonya sat back down next to me. "I overheard Granddaddy talking to Grandma last night."

"What did he say?"

"He told Granddaddy that he was coming to pick me and Jeffrey up earlier than planned."

"When?"

"In two weeks." Sonya leaned her head against my arm. "Don't think of it as leaving. Let's say we've been on vacation." She smiled.

"Sonya, how do you come up with a positive from such a negative?"

The thunder startled us. The boys ran home from across the field with their bats and the grocery bags they used for the bases. Tuffy and the Harris dog barked.

"Will you at least think about what I said?" I asked.

Sonya nodded.

"Maggie, here comes Mama, Uncle Ted and Aunt Louise," Mary said pointing.

Jeffrey had run home from the baseball field, but minutes later, rushed through our back door.

"You better be glad Mama didn't hear that door slam. They just drove into the driveway."

Mama came into the house with her purse over her head, hoping to stop the rain from getting to her hair. She sat her purse on the dining room table.

"Maggie. Help me look for the candles. If the lights go out, we'll need them."

"Grandpa sent me over to get Sonya before it rains," Jeffrey said.

Jeffrey tugged on her arm and pulled her to the door.

Chapter 13

Each day after I topped onions, Sonya and I spent every minute together. She'd call and ask if I'd eaten supper yet I always responded by saying yes and that I'd meet her on the front porch.

Sonya would skip along the dirt road and burst through the back door asking, "What do you want to do today?" Sometimes she'd help me wash the dishes after dinner or sweep.

If we didn't know what game to play, I'd make one up. Tonight we counted cars and trucks. Sonya looked to the left and me to the right. A truck counted for two points. A station wagon was one and a half points, and any other car was one point.

We heard squealing in the front yard to the side of the house. It sounded like it was coming from the tree by the picnic table.

Sonya and I ran. Tuffy and the neighbor dog were connected together from behind.

"Mike!" I yelled.

One dog was pulling in the opposite directions.

"Mike! Hurry," I yelled again.

He quickly ran out and pumped a bucket of water and tossed it on the dogs, and they separated.

Tuffy was squealing, wagging his tail between his legs. He ran underneath the house.

"What's wrong with Tuffy?" Mama asked running with Uncle Ted and Aunt Louise from their house. "We heard him squealing."

"Where did he go?" Uncle Ted asked.

Mike pointed underneath the house.

Uncle Ted kneeled down. "Come here boy," he said.

Tuffy hesitated.

Uncle Ted whistled for him. Tuffy came from underneath the house with his body rubbing the ground and his tail wagging.

"Oh, he'll be all right," Uncle Ted said rubbing his forehead.

"Maggie," Sonya said, "it's getting dark out. I'm supposed to be home before dusk."

"Okay. See you tomorrow." I went into the house.

* * *

Mary sat in the bedroom on the footstool in front of me while I braided her hair. I braided four braids in the back of her head and one across the top.

"Could you go and get some bobby-pins from the top of the dresser and your night rag?"

Mary came back with five bobby-pins and handed them to me. But before sitting back down she asked me a question. "Is Sonya really not coming back next summer? She's fun to be around and the two of you let me sit on the front porch, writing in my own diary."

"Don't worry about what you heard Sonya say. I'm sure she'll be back next year," I said. "Now, hand me your night rag."

While I wrapped Mary's head, Mama walked over to my side of the bed and sat next to me.

"Maggie, I couldn't help but hear you and your sister's conversation about Sonya. It's going to be all right."

"But what if she doesn't?"

"You do have friends."

"I know, but it's not the same as having my cousin visit."

Mama squeezed my shoulders. "It'll be all right."

I wrapped my night rag around my own braids and prayed that God would change Sonya's mind.

* * *

The morning that Cousin June Bug, Sonya and Jeffrey's daddy, arrived, he honked four times. Any time family arrived or left for a trip, they'd honk to the beat of the song on the radio or make up their own.

Mike came into our bedroom. "Mama, Cousin June Bug is here."

I hurried out of bed not wanting to believe it. I walked fast to the boy's bedroom to look out their window. He was right. As big as day Cousin June Bug's car was parked in Uncle John's driveway. This can't be the day Sonya goes home. Just yesterday, we were sitting in the oversized chair playing a game and listening to the boys argue over who was out or safe on base.

I went outside and stood beside the trees that separated

Uncle John's house from ours.

"Come here, pipsqueak," Cousin June Bug said to Sonya. "Boy, you've grown over the summer. Nothing but legs."

"Daddy, I like your new car! Another T-bird, huh?"

June Bug loved T-birds and dressed stylishly when he drove. Sonya had told me that she and her mama loved riding in the T-bird, the wind blowing against their faces, wearing silk head scarves.

I walked around the trees.

"Hey, Maggie," Cousin June Bug said. "Good to see you again."

"How are you gonna get everything inside that little car?" I asked. "Don't get me wrong, it's pretty and all."

"Well, I have another surprise." He walked to the end of the driveway and waved.

Another car—a station wagon—drove closer to the house.

"Mama!" Sonya jumped up and down.

"I wanted it to be a surprise," Sonya's mama, Cynthia, said when she got out of the car. She rarely came with June Bug to White Cloud.

Uncle John, Aunt Pearl, Jeffrey, and Sonya squeezed her until I thought she wouldn't be able to breathe.

"Are you guys leaving tomorrow?" I blurted out. Silence.

"Nah," Cousin June Bug said. "Not until Sunday."

I tried to smile but couldn't.

"I couldn't come all this way to leave tomorrow. It's a long drive. Plus, this will give you and Sonya a little more time together."

Aunt Pearl waved everyone to the house. I started to walk away. "That means you too, Maggie. You hungry?"

Everyone walked into the house together. Sonya and I waited for Aunt Pearl to ask us to set the table. She smiled but didn't say anything.

The phone rang. "Yes, he's here," Aunt Pearl said. "Sunday, after church. I'll talk to June Bug."

"You'll talk to me about what?" June Bug asked.

"Aunt Louise and the rest of the family want to cook dinner on Sunday. Typically, if we don't eat at the church, we all go over to her house after service."

"You know that I was going leave on Sunday," he said.

"June Bug, we can stay one more day," Cousin Cynthia said.

June Bug didn't look happy. He asked for some privacy.

Sonya and I leaned near the bedroom door where Cousin June Bug and Cousin Cynthia were talking.

"You know the ride back to Chicago is a long one and not many stops for coloreds, especially when riding in a red T-bird in rural areas. I'm already taking off work," he said. "Now I'll probably have to request another day."

"Just one more day, honey," Cousin Cynthia said.

Cousin June Bug let out a sigh. "Okay. At least tell me what we're having for dinner?"

"Come out of that room you two," Aunt Pearl said. "If you haven't made a decision about Sunday, you can make it later. You just arrived earlier today and it's time for supper."

The women cooked mashed potatoes, fried chicken, corn bread, string beans and sweet corn, fresh from the garden.

We listened to Mahalia Jackson on the record player. A cool breeze flowed through the window screen.

After the table was cleaned and the dishes were washed, Uncle John read from one of his many books.

Chapter 14

My alarm clock beeped. I rubbed the crust from my eyes and felt the mattress move.

My bedroom was semi-dark. Mama sat on the edge of the bed with her back toward Mary and me. She pushed the sheets aside and turned on the lamp that was on the dresser next to the bed. She stretched her arms to the ceiling and thanked Jesus for allowing her to wake up another day, something she did every morning.

Normally, I'd sleep until Mama shook me four or five times. But, most of the night, I tossed and turned thinking. Cousin Sonya would be leaving three weeks earlier.

It was another topping onion day, nothing to be excited about, so when Mama got up, I closed my eyes and pretended to be asleep.

I heard Mike's and Edward's voices from the back of the house fussing about the list of chores on the refrigerator. Edward felt that he had more than last week.

During the school year, they shared responsibilities.

Edward made the lunches and school bus watch assignments. This meant he assigned which of the brothers or myself looked out for the bus so we wouldn't miss it. Mike made sure Joe was dressed and walked him and Mary to Mrs. Ollie's house before school. I was responsible for getting Mary dressed.

"Edward," Mama said, "make sure the car is packed with lunches and blankets. Last time the blankets got left and we had to sit in the dirt."

"The lunches, water, and Kool-Aid are all in the coolers, Mama," Edward said.

"And the blank-"

"The blankets and sheets are already in the car."

"Are the twins stayin' with Mrs. Ollie today?" Mike asked.

"No," Mama said. "They're coming with us. Make sure they have their hats. And grab two more of those old blankets in the storage room for them to sit on when they wake up."

When my brothers finished loading the car, Mike let Mama know that it was misty outside.

"Hmmm," Mama said.

I knew that meant we were still going to work.

It had rained last night. Mama and Aunt Louise walked to the road in front of our house to check its condition. If it was too wet outside, that meant that the muck was wet with puddles and we wouldn't have to top onions.

Mike went with them.

The rest of us looked out our front porch windows. Aunt Louise tapped her foot against the dirt road. Mike stepped on Aunt Louise's footprints. They stood outside for ten minutes.

Mama came into the house. "We're still going to the fields," Mama announced. "We'll have to drive carefully to not get stuck in the road."

Once the decision was made to top onions, Aunt Louise and Lewis, her foster child got into her car. There wasn't room in our station wagon for everyone. Mama drove the lead car.

The closer we got to the fields, the more we smelled the onions. The misty rain worsened the smell. Our choices were to roll the windows down or to contend with the smell from our onion-smelling clothes. No matter how many times we washed our work clothes, the onion smell lingered.

I chose to roll down the window.

Mama drove around the bend. The mist lessened. "I hope I don't hit that hole on this road," she said. "I can't afford any car repairs." The hole had caused damage to a number of cars.

The entire car shook as Mama drove on the road alongside the muck, waking the rest of our family.

Mama and Aunt Louise parked the cars and began to get out. The field chief pointed back to the direction where we had entered. I smiled and began to get excited, thinking we didn't have to work today. Mama walked back to the car and drove as if we were going home, but then veered to the left. Between a patch of tall trees, I saw more fields. The smile on my face vanished. My shoulders slumped.

Our family was assigned to the front field. We'd be away from Lucy, a little girl I'd gotten to know over the last month.

We got out of the car. These fields were larger than the others.

"I see why he changed fields," Mama said.

"Yes," Aunt Louise said. "These fields aren't as close to the swampy areas in the back and aren't around as many trees. They're not as damp."

Mama and Aunt Louise divided the rows among the seven of us. The twins were still asleep, and Mama decided to leave them in the car until they woke up. It was Mike's responsibility to check on them every half hour, although at times, Mama did. Normally, the twins stayed with Mrs. Ollie, but she and Aunt Pearl had a doctor appointment today.

The fifth time Mike walked back to the car, the twins had awakened. They ran down the rows while Mike carried their blankets. Mama waved for him to bring the blankets to her and Aunt Louise. He spread the blankets across the areas where they had already topped onions.

Mary wanted to be near me. Mama stood up with her hands on her hips. She was further up the rows than me. "Maggie, do you think you can watch Mary and top?"

"Yes ma'am," I answered. I pointed my finger at Mary. "Mary, you have to stay close to me. Do you understand?"

She nodded.

"We can make up games, or I can tell you some of my stories."

Mary enjoyed listening to my stories. If I didn't make up one, I'd find one of our books that Uncle John gave us.

"Could you tell me a story today?"

"Mary, we don't have any books."

"Can you read from my coloring book?"

"I have to keep topping the onions."

"Can you make up a story while you top?"

"You're a persistent little girl."

The only thing I could think of was the fields, sky, smell of onions, and families.

"This story begins with 'The families drove down a two-track dirt road with anticipation of seeing more onions. Each family was to be assigned to a different field, but when they got out of their cars, there weren't onions."

"What did they see?" Maggie asked.

"The families got out of their cars and were amazed.

The muck felt like black silk as the families let it sift through their hands. The stems were the purest green and sparkled. They were attached to onions, but they were golden and had no smell."

"These smell." Maggie frowned.

"The fields were further than their eyes could see. The families wondered why the fields didn't have the odor of onions."

"Why?" Maggie asked.

"Well, the farmer was tired of the smell and the complaints, so he sprayed a sweet scent all over his onions. The families didn't complain, and their clothes didn't stink. The end."

"That was a beautiful story, Maggie. I liked it."

I noticed that the sky was a pretty blue, not cloudy anymore and the sun shined down on us.

"Maggie?"

"Yes."

"Will I have to top onions?"

Sheers in hand, I grasped the top of the crate. "Maybe."

Mary tried to grab onto an onion stem, but I brushed it away from her.

With a concerned voice, I said, "I didn't mean to scare you, but if you get the juice in your eyes, it will sting."

"Sorry."

"Where's your coloring book? Show me some of your coloring."

Mary flipped the pages.

"Oh, Mary, how beautiful. Color some more while I top these onions."

Usually, our families worked until five o'clock, but today I had an appointment with Doc Douglas.

Mama and Aunt Louise walked over to the field chief.

Before he counted our crates, he lifted his cap to wipe the sweat from his forehead with a handkerchief. He counted our topped onion crates and wrote a number on a piece of paper. After doing the math, I heard him tell Mama and Aunt Louise to meet him at his truck.

Mama counted the money. "This is less today, but it's something," she told Aunt Louise.

"We'll do better next time," Aunt Louise said.

While Mama and Aunt Louise talked with the field chief, Mike, Edward, Thomas, and I looked at each other. No words were necessary.

"Mary," I said, "when you see me run, run as fast as you can behind me. I want to sit in the front or by a window."

"Maggie, slow down," she yelled.

Mike ran with Joe in his arms.

Edward and Thomas yelled, "Maggie, we get to sit by the windows."

Who sat by the windows seemed to be an ongoing feud between my brothers and I. At times, we'd stand outside the car until Mama decided. Whoever touched the car first sat by the front window.

Edward grabbed the door handle on one side of the car and Mike second. By the time Thomas reached the car, there was only a middle spot left behind the front seat. After he whined about how unfair everything was and kicked at the muck dirt, he sat in between Edward and Mike.

Aunt Louise followed Mama from the fields until it connected with the main road.

As we got closer to home, I turned around in my seat and pretended to joke with Joe. It was a decoy to see if my brothers were sleep or not because I knew there was going to be a mad dash to the bathroom.

Mama slowed down to make the turn into the driveway.

Gravel crunched under the tires. I leaned against the door and held the handle, ready to open it. I turned my head a little to see Thomas and Edward trying to look over the front seat to see what I was up to.

As soon as Mama stopped the car, I dashed toward the front door of the house.

"Shoot!" Edward hollered. "Maggie's beating us again."

"Edward," Mama yelled, "you almost slammed the door on your little brother's fingers."

"But Mama—"

"But Mama nothing."

I rushed to the tub.

"You and Mary can use the same bath water," Mama said.

Mary stood behind Mama and peeked at me.

"But she didn't top any onions," I said.

"Let her take a bath anyway."

I rolled my eyes. Mary waited with me until the tub was full. "Come on, get in," I said. "Hope you don't mind the smell of onion water."

We sat in the tub and tried to make bubbles into different shapes. Mary mimicked me. When I cleaned my toes, laid the washcloth on my forehead, and cleaned my fingernails, she did the same. We stayed in the bath until the onion smell of my clothes on the floor became unbearable.

Uncle John, Uncle Ted, and Mike had built a small bathroom closet with spare two-by-fours and plywood left in Uncle Ted's shed. There wasn't a door.

Mama came into the bathroom with the linen. "Maggie, from now on, you can put the toilet paper, towels, and bed sheets in here."

I reached for two towels. "Come on Mary. Sonya will

be over soon."

After all of the supplies were on the shelves, Mary and I went into our bedroom.

Sonya walked into the house and, as usual, hollered my name. "Maggie! Are you dressed yet?"

"I'm in my bedroom." I tried to sound happy even though Sonya and Jeffrey's two-month vacation would come to an end after the family dinner tomorrow.

"I'll be on the front porch," Sonya said.

By the time I got to the porch, Sonya had set up the checkerboard. I reached inside my pocket and unfolded our summer to-do list, but Sonya acted as if the list didn't exist and shied away, wanting to play Checkers instead.

I folded the list and put it back inside my pocket. We played two games of Checkers. I didn't say anything.

We were in the middle of the third game when Sonya said, "Can I tell you another secret?" She leaned against the back of the chair.

"Yes." I hesitated to place my checker.

Sonya was quiet.

"Well, are you gonna tell me or not?" I asked.

Sonya lowered her head.

"If I put my checker piece here," I said, "you'll do this. And if I put it here—"

Sonya blurted out, "I have a boyfriend!"

I dropped the checker piece on the board. "What?"

"Mama doesn't know."

"A real boyfriend?"

"Well, we haven't kissed or anything."

"Does that make him a boyfriend, then?"

Sonya paused to think. "Why not? We hold hands and sit on his steps."

"I guess that makes him a boyfriend. That's a good last

secret for the summer."

"No. You mean to tell me you waited until the end of summer to tell me this?" I asked

"I don't know why I waited. I-I. Well, you know now."

"What about you?" Sonya asked.

I shuffled my feet around on the floor. Avoiding the subject, I asked what she wanted to do next.

"You do, don't you?" Sonya moved up and down in the chair with her hands over her mouth.

I took a deep breath and told Sonya, "His family lives across town. We visit them from time-to-time."

"Maggie, does your Mama know?"

"No way." I wrinkled my forehead. "And right now it's a crush, I think."

"Have you told him?"

"For God's sake, no."

The floor creaked.

Mike held onto the corner of the wall with one hand. "Sonya, your Grandma wants to talk to you on the phone."

Sonya left. When she came back to the front porch, she said, "I have to get home. Grandma wants me to help with dinner."

"What are you having?" I asked. "If it sounds tasty, I'll see if I can come over."

"Hamburgers, corn on the cob, and Kool-Aid."

Aunt Pearl's dinner sounded much better than pork 'n beans with cut up hotdogs.

Sonya and I rushed into my bedroom. Mama sat in a chair, reading her Bible.

Before we could ask her, Mama said, "I heard you from the front porch. But don't be late after dinner. We have church—"

"I know, in the morning," I said.

Right now I wasn't thinking about church. I was thinking, No beans and cut up hotdogs tonight!

Sonya and I ran out of the house and up the footpath.

I sang, "Sonya has a boyfriend."

"And Maggie has, well, something," Sonya sang.

Once we got halfway up the footpath, we slowed to a walk. "Sonya, that's our last secret for the summer."

"I should feel sad, but I don't. I miss Chicago and the city smells." She looked at me. "I mean, I'll miss you, but... but not White Cloud."

Sonya claimed not to like White Cloud, but deep inside, I didn't believe that. She'll be back next summer, I thought, no matter how bad the hogs and chickens smell.

Chapter 15

Sunday morning, I was excited and sad at the same time. After dinner last night, Sonya and I had agreed to wear something alike.

Today, there was a change in our parade of cars going to church. Uncle Ted waited in his driveway for Aunt Louise honking his horn. We sat in our car when I noticed Mama looking at her watch. Uncle John was also late, fifteen minutes. Uncle John drove his car, but followed behind Cousin Cynthia and Cousin June Bug in their car. They lined up alongside our house and parked.

Aunt Louise finally came out from the house and we drove across White Cloud into the church parking lot. When Sonya and I entered the church, I spit on my hands and wiped away any dirt. To my surprise, Sonya, the city girl did the same thing.

Sonya sat in the back of the church. I gathered in the back room with the choir.

Mama hit one key on the piano, which was the cue for

the choir to line up on each side of the church, the men on the right and the women on the left. She stood up and raised her left hand, again playing one note continuously with her right hand. The choir stood in place.

The choir didn't have choir robes because they were too expensive, but Mama was proud that everyone had the same uniform. Today the choir wore the usual black and white ensemble. I wore my white laced socks and black patent leather shoes. Sonya's shoes had a strap with a button, and mine were slip-ons, but close enough.

When the church service was over, I rushed to Cheryl's house. "Cheryl, I can't stay today," I told her. "Sonya's leaving tomorrow, and our family has prepared supper."

When I looked behind me, I saw Sonya sitting in the car. Uncle John had moved it to the back of the church near the kitchen. There were two chairs that needed to be fixed, and he put them inside his trunk.

"See you next Sunday," I said to Cheryl.

When we got home, Tuffy came out from underneath the house wagging his tail, happy to see us. The chickens clucked and the pigs grunted.

Mama told us, "Keep your Sunday clothes on, and don't go near the animals. And Maggie, please don't rip your dress climbing trees. Mike, you and Edward can go over to our house and bring the cakes."

Aunt Louise's house smelled like Thanksgiving. After prayer, we ate and listened to gospel music, family jokes, and stories. Then we changed our clothes and played baseball.

Uncle Ted was the catcher for one team, and Uncle John was the catcher for the other team. Aunt Pearl, June Bug, Cynthia, Sonya, and Jeffrey played too. The twins kept score.

After the game, some of the kids sat in the wooden

swing in the front yard. The grownups clustered on and around Uncle Ted's front porch.

Uncle Ted told us a story of when he was a hobo and traveled on trains. We laughed when he talked about how he and Aunt Louise met in Woodland Park, Michigan, not because it was funny, but because none of us knew why a sweet man like Uncle Ted had married a stern woman like Aunt Louise.

The next day, June Bug, Cynthia, Sonya, and Jeffrey put their luggage inside their two cars.

The adults stood on the back porch of Uncle John's house and waved good-bye. The kids, even Lewis, ran to the end of the driveway and up the road a few feet.

"See you next year!" People hollered.

When I turned around it was the Harris boys running down the road past our house, waving their arms in the air. They stopped when they reached Uncle John's house.

Sonya rode with her mama. Jeffrey rode with his daddy, who honked repeatedly while driving, as if he was playing a song.

Jeffrey leaned out of an opened window and waved. "See you next year...maybe!"

"Boy, sit down in that car before you fall out!" Uncle John yelled.

Sonya waved from her car window. She didn't say, "See you next year!" Her mama started honking the horn too. Dust from the gravel road stirred up behind the car wheels.

I stood at the end of the driveway until the dust settled and whispered, "See you next year."

Mama surprised me when she put her arm around my shoulder. "Are you all right?"

"Mama, I know I've said this many times, but Sonya... Mama, she felt like another sister to me."

"I know, but soon you'll be back in school and with the

rest of your friends."

With my hands in both pockets, I walked up the footpath and kicked into the dirt. I sat on the front porch in the oversized chair that Sonya and I had sat in for the past two months.

"Can I sit next to you?" Mary asked.

"Sure." I patted a spot on the chair.

"Do you want to play Checkers?"

"No, let's just sit."

Chapter 16

Two weeks had passed since Sonya had left. I leaned against the car in my pressed church dress and waited for the rest of the family, thinking about Sonya. I wondered how and what she was doing.

Sonya was right—the chickens, pigs, and other country odors stunk. The smells had never bothered me until Sonya had complained about them.

I'd lived here for so long and traveled nowhere except to Fremont and Baldwin. That was to make us think we'd gone somewhere and to have something to talk about other than picking the farmers' crops when our teachers asked us what we did all summer.

"Ted!" Aunt Louise yelled, interrupting my thoughts. "Hurry up and get in the car. We're going to be late opening the church doors."

I missed Sonya and seeing Jeffrey sit in the backseat waving his long arms spastically out the window.

When we reached our church, we saw Deacon Samuel's

car. The church windows were already opened.

"I'm sorry for being late," Uncle Ted said to Deacon Samuel.

Deacon Samuel gave him a firm hand shake. "No matter. The only thing left is the pastor's office and pulpit area."

There were voices in the kitchen.

"Maggie, follow me and your aunts to the kitchen," Mama said.

Sister Patterson and Sister Jones sat at one of the round tables, looking at a piece of paper. "Praise the Lord," Mama and my aunts said.

"This is the food we'll be serving today," Sister Jones said.

I sat near them, but at a corner table.

Sister Patterson pointed. "See here? I checked off the collard greens. I cooked them last night in that big pot over there."

"And I put a check mark here next to the yams that I cooked." Sister Jones pointed.

"After the choir sings, I can come and help prepare the corn bread," Mama said.

"I brought mac and cheese," Aunt Pearl said. "I'll just set it next to the stove. I can heat it up before the service ends."

"I can finish making mashed potatoes," Aunt Louise said.

Sister Patterson and Sister Jones went through the list, checking off more items as church members brought them in.

There were three cakes, five sweet potato pies, and several apple pies on the counter.

"Who's going to fry the chicken?" Mama asked.

"Not sure, but someone will during the church service," Sister Jones said. "The seasoned mix is ready and the chicken is cut up. The sanctuary door can be cracked open so that we won't miss someone else bringing food in the back door."

"The kitchen shouldn't be a distraction," Aunt Pearl said. "We have to be as quiet as possible while in the kitchen."

Mama, Sister Jones, and Sister Patterson went over the rest of the after-service food list before leaving it on the counter.

The Saginaw Church of God in Christ was visiting our church, so last Sunday, Pastor Johnson had decided that today's services would be shortened.

An hour before services, the parking lot was so full that people began to park alongside the road, across from the church in Pastor Johnson's driveway, and beyond the apple tree in the back yard behind the church.

It was hot inside the sanctuary, and there weren't enough hand fans to go around. The deacons had put two tall, metal fans in the back corners of the church. All six windows were pushed up, but there was not enough wind.

The two choirs mixed together. The Saginaw choir from Pastor Beattie's church was larger and had choir robes. Both choir directors lead the choirs for one song each.

Fortunately for me, I had a cold and didn't have to sing today. I sat in the back row, first seat.

Pastor Johnson stood. "Everyone, please stand and welcome our combined choirs."

The Saginaw choir stood in the back of the church in one aisle, and our choir stood in the other, waiting for the choir directors' signals. Mama hit one key on the piano and looked toward Sister Evelyn, the choir director from Saginaw. She lifted her left hand and their choir began to clap. Then our choir spread their arms and clapped even louder, so loud that the claps echoed. I'm quite sure that if Cheryl was outside, she heard it too.

The congregation, which had hesitated to stand, got to its feet, clapped, and yelled, "Go, head choirs."

The choirs marched in place, moving side-to-side. The sopranos started with their solos, and then the baritones, altos, and bass singers joined in. The choirs marched down the center aisle, intertwined.

No matter who we sang with, I always thought that our choir sounded the best. But when both choirs sang together, it felt like I had gone to heaven.

"Mama's gonna get you for sitting back here during church service," Edward said. "You'd better move up front before she sees you."

I leaned backward in the chair and looked up. It was Edward. He signaled with his head to the front of the church, but I didn't move. I stood with the rest of the church and rubbed the petticoat marks on the back of my legs.

When our church choir went to the choir stand, Pastor Johnson motioned for the congregation to sit down.

Before singing their A selection, Mama looked left and then right throughout the congregation. Our eyes met. She pointed for me to come sit in the first seat in the front row.

At times during the summer, Mama had let me sit in the back row with Sonya. We'd giggle, waiting to see whose petticoat raised their dresses the highest.

I rubbed my butt against the wooden seat and frowned, not only because I had to sit up front, but also because of the marks my petticoat had left on my legs. It seemed like Mama counted my every step until I sat down in the front seat.

Whenever a guest church visited, I always prayed for services to end sooner. But, to me the visiting pastor was as long-winded as Pastor Johnson, which didn't help any with the petticoat I wore.

I twitched in the seat left and right, forward and

backward, trying to get comfortable, but so far, my petticoat was winning. Numbness settled in my legs.

"Wake up, sis," Mike said.

"You better thank God that Mama had to help in the kitchen," Edward said. "She'd never let us fall asleep in church."

"Oh hush up," I brushed Edward away with my hand. "My goodness that food smells good."

Mike gestured for Thomas, Mary, and Joe to come up front of the line with the rest of the family.

Our church wasn't that big and the kitchen even smaller. I'd move forward as the line moved smelling the fried chicken and collard greens.

"Finally," I said.

Guests were first to eat. The kitchen was crowded and a few seats remained. I noticed a seat left at my favorite table, the one near the window and door.

Mama scooped a spoonful of mac and cheese. "The deacons pulled out the picnic tables from the church garage. You kids can sit out there near the apple tree away from the cars."

"Yes, ma'am," Mike said.

We watched the missionaries add chairs around the tables.

"Mike," Mama said. "Please watch the smaller kids. And Maggie and Mary, please don't get those dresses dirty."

I hurried to finish my food and Kool-Aid when I saw Cheryl feeding her chickens.

As soon as I was done eating, I ran to Cheryl's fence. She had just climbed over it when Mama called from the church kitchen, "Maggie, remember what I told you about that dress."

"Okay," I shouted.

Other kids played tag, but I didn't. I loved climbing the large apple tree. It had perfect branches. The limbs spread from one to the other, enough for me to stretch my legs. Some Sundays, I'd reach the top of the tree and sit in the branches that were like a glove.

"Maggie, why are there so many cars in the church's parking lot today?" Cheryl asked.

"A church from Saginaw is fellowshipping with us today."

"Oh." Cheryl looked around. "Where's your cousin?"

"Her daddy came and picked her up last week. He took her and Jeffrey back to Chicago."

"I thought—"

"She was supposed to stay until the end of summer, only a few more weeks, but that all changed."

Cheryl began to climb the tree, but I stopped her.

"Let's do something else," I said.

We talked about going back to school and watched the chickens fight.

Cheryl asked if I wanted to race to the woods and back.

"What about all the cars?" I asked.

"The race is to weave in between them and back."

I leaned forward.

"On your mark," Cheryl said. "Get set—"

"Go!" I yelled.

I ran ahead of her, but within seconds, she passed me. The tall weeds brushed against our legs. Cheryl touched the tree and turned around it. My feet got tangled up trying to go around the cars and into the bushes by the trees. I fell.

"I won," Cheryl said holding her arms up in the air.

I pushed myself up off the ground and saw a dirty spot on my dress.

"Maggie?"

The voice startled me. I stood up and looked for any scratches on my legs.

"Maggie?"

I rushed through the bushes. Edward. Darn it. Why couldn't it be Mike? I thought.

Edward looked up and down at my dress and at my scratches.

"Please don't tell Mama," I said.

He stood there like a police officer with his arms crossed.

"Please, Edward," I pleaded.

"Let me think about what you can do for me."

I've died and gone to hell, I thought.

Edward and I spit on our hands and wiped at the scratches on my legs. Thank God my dress didn't have any rips in it. I would have to explain the dirty spot. I could tell Mama that someone had pushed me.

"You'll help me with my chores," Edward said. "Deal?"

"Let me think."

"Well?"

"Okay." I frowned. "Deal."

"See you later, Cheryl," I said. "We have to go."

Mama opened the kitchen screen door. Before she could see me, I darted in another direction around the church and leaned out.

"Didn't you hear me call your name?" She asked.

"I was near the front of the church when Edward told me you were calling for me."

I looked back at Edward. He smiled like he was winning.

Although I didn't trust that he wouldn't tell Mama, I also had a secret. He didn't know that I saw him stealing penny candy from the Walton's grocery store in town.

Chapter 17

I woke up early and tiptoed to the dresser for my diary, hoping not to wake up Mary. Mama had already gone to work. I sat in the chair next to our bedroom window and began to write.

> *School will start in a few days. There will be something else besides picking crops...*

I heard voices in the living room and moved the curtains back. Mike and Edward were sitting across from each other in the living room.

"Shhh," I said. "Mary's sleeping."

"She has to get up anyway. Remember?" Mike said.

"I know, but..." Mike was right. Mama had gone to work and left instructions his piano lesson is later today.

Mary sat up in the bed. "What's all the fussin'?"

"Mike and Edward arguing," I said. "It's time to get up anyway." She stumbled while putting on her house shoes and grabbed onto my arm. We began to walk out of the bedroom.

She looked up at me. "Soon Joe and I will be in school, and it won't be a practice like now."

Joe sat next to Mary and me at the table and waited for breakfast. Thomas sat down, crossed his arms, and rested his head.

Edward finished cooking the last of the powdered eggs, the ones that came with our box of welfare food. I hated them. They tasted like cardboard.

"Can I have some corn flakes instead?" I asked.

"No," Edward said. "You have to eat what I cook." He pointed to the monthly menu Mama had taped on the refrigerator next to the list of chores.

I frowned. "I'll eat the toast."

It was silent until Mike tapped on the table with his fork. "There was a slight change to the chores." He removed the list from the refrigerator. "Thomas, you'll have to finish folding the laundry. Maggie, you'll have to make sure the dining room table is cleaned."

"We have to finish all of our chores or we won't be able to go to the Labor Day parade in town, right?" I asked.

"Right," Mike said, "so if everyone is finished eating, we can start our chores, at least those that aren't already done. That way, when Aunt Louise comes over, we'll be done."

Mike taped the list back to the refrigerator. I followed him to double-check what I had to do. Mike and Edward had already put a line through the completed chores. While I was checking the list, Edward frantically walked out of his bedroom and bumped into me on his way to the bathroom.

He came out hollering, "Mike! Thomas! Have you seen my dark blue shorts? The ones with the big pockets on the side? Last night when I checked, they were in my drawer."

Mike yelled, "No" from the bedroom.

Thomas didn't say a word. He slurped his milk.

Edward went back into the bedroom. He told Mike, "I know. I put them right here in my drawer."

"Thomas!" I called.

No response. He slurped what appeared to be an empty glass of milk.

Edward came out of the room. He stood at the head of the dining room table, staring at Thomas. Then he sat down and extended his hands gripping the corners. "Thomas, it was you, wasn't it?"

"What you talkin' about?" Thomas said in an innocent voice.

Edward stood and shoved his chair back.

Mike ran out of the bedroom. "Edward, calm down," he said. "Thomas, did you move Edward's shorts? Don't lie."

Thomas sat back in his chair. He looked around the table at the three of us. "I didn't move them. Maybe Edward misplaced them."

It didn't seem like Edward believed him.

"Just put on some different shorts," Mike told Edward. "Remember that if we don't get our chores done in two hours, none of us will be able to go to the parade."

Edward still didn't look happy but worked on his chores.

Mary and I washed the dishes. Joe and Thomas swept the living room and kitchen floors. Edward cleaned the bathroom and helped Thomas fold the clothes that were tossed in the corner of the linen area. Mike dumped the garbage and fed the animals. Everyone worked frantically and put a line through each chore they completed.

Edward ran out of the bathroom and yelled, "My shorts!" He held them up in the air as if he had won a prize.

Mary and I stopped cleaning the living room and ran into the dining room. Edward's smile spread across his face.

Thomas walked into the dining room and shoved a chair out of his way. It toppled to the floor. He grabbed the shorts from Edward's hand. "Are these the shorts you accused me of taking?

"The shorts were—"

Aunt Louise knocked on the door and let herself in. She asked sternly, "What you kids fussing about?"

Mike stuttered, "Nothing." He picked up the chair and changed the subject to the parade.

"Well, is everyone ready to go in town?" Aunt Louise asked.

Mary and I ran to get our jackets. The boys grabbed their baseball caps.

Mama had to work today and had told Aunt Louise she'd meet up with everyone when she finished.

Aunt Pearl had a station wagon, everyone rode with her to town. As usual, the boys tussled in the backseat, hitting each other.

Aunt Louise turned halfway around in the front seat. "Edward and Thomas, stop that foolishness or I'm telling Pearl to stop this car so I can get a switch."

The boys immediately settled down, but not without mocking Aunt Louise' words.

The White Cloud city limits were seven miles from where we lived, but we had the choice of taking M-37 or Wilson into town. M-37 ran between the front of a private airport and the forest station near town. Wilson was on the opposite side of the airport, a roller coaster-type hill.

When we were less than a half-mile from Wilson, I tapped Aunt Pearl's shoulder. In a pitiful voice, I asked, "Could you turn right onto Wilson?"

Aunt Louise gave me that don't bother your auntie while she's driving expression.

I scooted back in my seat. Aunt Pearl adjusted the rearview mirror and made eye contact with me. She smiled.

As Aunt Pearl drove up the hill, Lewis, my siblings and I held our arms halfway up, as if we were on a roller coaster. When the car went down the hill, I held onto my stomach. Going down the hill always made it feel squeamish.

Aunt Pearl drove slowly behind the line of cars nearing Doc Douglas' office on the corner of Elm and Wilson. When a clown rushed up to the car, she slammed on the brakes. Aunt Louise grabbed Mary's shoulders so that she wouldn't hit the dashboard.

"Would you kids like a balloon?" the clown asked. None of us recognized his voice until he apologized. "Sorry, Miss Pearl and Miss Louise."

"Hank!" Aunt Louise frowned.

Mr. Hank, as the kids called him, was the school janitor.

"Aunt Pearl, can I have a balloon?" Mary asked, bouncing up and down in her seat.

"Can I have one too?" Joe asked.

"Yes," Aunt Pearl said.

Joe stretched his arms from the backseat for a balloon. Aunt Pearl handed one to him and to Mary.

As Mr. Hank stepped away from the car, Aunt Louise leaned forward, wiggling her index finger. "Hank, please don't scare the next car full of kids."

Mr. Henderson, who lived in town, stood in the middle of the street and directed us to available parking spaces. "Keep moving," he said, waving his arms at the traffic.

We passed the Catholic Church. The high school band instructor stood on the church's sidewalk. When he lifted his arms, the band started to practice a song.

Joe's balloon swayed into my face. I pushed it aside. "You better hold onto that darn balloon before I pop it."

I leaned out the car window and saw girls with their batons, the ones who marched in front of the band, practicing. They turned in circles as they tossed their batons in the air.

"When I'm in high school, I'm gonna ask Mama if I can twirl a baton with the band," I mumbled.

"You'll have to learn how to march in place, twirl in a circle, and toss your baton up in the air," Edward said. "You already trip and fall over your feet just walkin'." He chuckled.

"And?" I said.

"You'll still have to catch it, right?"

"Just wait and see."

Edward continued to tease me, but I ignored him. My eyes were mesmerized by the girls tossing batons in the air. Some girls caught them. Other batons slipped out of the girls' hands and fell to the ground.

On the street to the right of the band, the floats lined up. Every year each high school class designed a float.

My favorite parts of the parade were the floats that carried each high school queen, the baton girls, and the drummers in the band. They played with such precision, not missing a beat.

Aunt Pearl turned into the next parking lot.

"Do you kids remember your mama's instructions that she gave to me and Pearl?" Aunt Louise asked. She turned around. "Did you kids hear me?"

I guess we hadn't answered fast enough. "Yes, ma'am. We remember."

"Mike and Edward, your mama told us that you could hang around your friends, but you have to be back near us by the time the parade starts," Aunt Louise said.

Thomas, Joe, Mary, and I had to stay with Aunt Louise and Aunt Pearl. We sat a little ways from the corner where the parade was to begin.

After we were there a half-hour, a man walked down the middle of the street hollering, "The parade will start in five minutes. Everyone, please clear the street."

Mike and Edward stood behind me. Thomas, Joe, Mary, and I were sitting on the curb when I heard someone call, "Hey, Maggie!"

Cheryl waved her arms from across the street. She was sitting with her family.

Mama had left strict instructions with Aunt Louise for my brothers, sister, and me to stay with Aunt Louise until Mama got off work and was able to join us.

"You can't cross the street," Aunt Louise said, "but your friend is more than welcome to come and sit with us if it's all right with her parents."

I waved to Cheryl and saw her whisper into her mama's ear. Her mama looked across the street and waved. Cheryl dashed across the street to join us.

Minutes later, the clowns, who always began the parade, came around the corner and tossed candy. Kids and some grownups bumped into each other, picking up the candy and putting it inside bags or pockets.

Soon, we saw convertibles with the homecoming queens. They half-smiled, barely blinked, and waved stiffly, like their fingers were glued together.

I asked Cheryl, "Can those cars move any slower?"

"They are going slow," Cheryl said. "The band will be here soon."

Mama walked up behind us. "Hello."

I turned away from the parade when Mama hugged all of us. "I assumed you all did your chores since you're at the parade," Mama asked.

Cheryl poked my side. But, it was too late. Raymond, the one I had a crush on and who walked with the 4-H Club had passed by us. All I saw was his back.

I heard the White Cloud High School band and stood up. It wasn't a large band, nor did everyone march in an exact processional line like I'd seen on the Thanksgiving Day Parade on the television, but it was our band.

"See the girls turning the batons?" I asked Cheryl. "I want to do that when I'm in high school."

My excitement grew when the drum section marched in place in front of me. I stared as the drumsticks hit the drums, flew up in the air, and were caught by the drummers.

The big circular drum seemed too heavy to carry. The weight of it tilted a boy's body backward. I felt sorry for him having to carry the monstrous thing. He moved his arms as far back as possible, and then with all his might, he hit the sticks against the drum, making a loud booming that echoed.

Finally, the mayor's car turned the corner. He waved to each side of the crowd, a big smile on his face.

When the parade ended, people scattered on Main Street. Some visited the stores while others met with their family members who had participated in the parade.

Jackie, Sarah, Cheryl and my other friends were supposed to meet us at the beginning of the parade. The four of us wandered around until we found Raymond, who was in a crowd of his friends. Raymond and I talked a little until Jackie tapped my shoulder. "I have to go find my mama."

Sarah, Cheryl, and I decided that we should also find our mama's and meet back at the Ferris wheel.

Cheryl and I caught up with her mama and daddy on Peach Street.

"How are you doing, Maggie?" Cheryl's mama asked.

"Good," I said.

"I spoke to your mother just a minute ago. You can meet her at the hardware store."

"Thank you. See you at school, Cheryl."

When I got to the hardware store, Mama was telling the owner that winter would be here soon and that our house was in need of pipes for underneath the kitchen sink.

It seemed like there was always something wrong either inside or outside our house.

"What's wrong now, Mama?" I asked.

Anytime she didn't want us kids to know, she'd change the subject. "How did you like the parade?" she asked.

"It wasn't too different from last year, except Raymond walked with the 4-H Club."

Mama smiled in a way that left me curious.

Mama and I walked around the corner from the hardware store and met the rest of the family at the beach in White Cloud. That's where the carnival was held each year.

"Come closer, kids," Mama said. She pulled her coin purse out of her pocket. "Mike, remember to help Joe on the rides. This should be enough money for both of you."

Mama turned toward Edward and Thomas and pointed her finger. "You two know what I'm about to say, but let me remind you again." She had a stern face. "Please don't spend all of your money in one place, and no fussing, arguing, or getting mad at the games if you don't win a prize."

Edward and Thomas frowned.

"Aunt Louise and Aunt Pearl will watch you both to make sure none of what I just said happens until I join them. You hear me?"

"Yes, ma'am," they both mumbled.

"Maggie, I know you want to run around with your friends, but take Mary with you." Mama paused. "I know she's younger and you feel like you're a big girl, entering fifth grade this year, but because you're a big girl, I know you can do this."

"But Mama..." I saw a pitiful look on Mary's face. "Okay," I said to Mary. "Besides, all of my friends like you."

"Maggie!" Cheryl, Jackie, and Sarah were waiting for me by the Ferris wheel.

"Go on," Mama said. "I'm going sit over there on that bench with your aunts."

My friends and I rode most of the rides except the Ferris wheel. I was afraid to go around in a circle up in the air. I watched Mary ride the kiddie rides. Jackie was the only one who was bothered that Mary came with us. She thought Mary would slow down our fun and that the boys wouldn't want to talk to us when we were with an almost five year old. Jackie staggered behind us. But, Jackie's hormones were getting the best of her. She smiled at most boys. By the end of day, we were tired from the rides, eating cotton candy, hotdogs and soda pop.

Mama saw Mary and me. "It's time to go home," she said. Joe sat next to Mama, leaning against her shoulder.

Mary ran in front of me. Joe was sitting next to Mama, leaned against her shoulders.

While we walked to the car, Mama asked, "Did you girls hang out with boys?"

I didn't know what to say. Mama had caught me off guard. She'd never asked me about boys before.

"No," I said. "Why are you asking me about boys?"

"Believe it or not, I was your age once." She smiled.

"Mama, no need to worry. I'm too young to think about boys," I lied.

Chapter 18

The squeaky mattress springs woke me. I rubbed my eyes. Mama sat on the bed, fastening her bra.

The lamp on the dresser was turned on, but Mama had placed a handkerchief over the top to help dim the room.

As I watched her stand up to put her white work uniform on, I began to think about how hard she worked to keep a roof over our heads, food on the table, and clothes on our backs. Why can't Daddy come back and help make everything all right again? I wondered.

She walked to the bedroom curtain and shoved it aside stopping. "Maggie," Mama whispered, "have a blessed first day at school today."

I never fooled her when I pretended to still be asleep. We both smiled.

Before Mama left, she always gave instructions to Mike. "Remember, Mike," she said, "to make sure that your brothers and sisters are up on time to catch the bus."

The back door shut.

I tossed off the covers, hurried to the bedroom window, and watched Mama turn out the driveway, headed in the direction of the Fremont where she worked in the nursing facility. Instead of getting back in bed, I sat in a chair next to the window, pulled a blanket halfway over me, and fell asleep.

I was in the middle of a dream when Mike shook me and told me to wake up. At first, I thought it was part of my dream.

"Maggie, wake up," Mike kept saying.

I had heard those words so much over the past months that it started to seem like my name had changed to Maggie Wake Up instead of Maggie Dorsey.

"Okay, okay," I said.

"We can't be late for the school bus, and I have to take Mary and Joe to Mrs. Ollie's house."

When I thought about it being the first day of school, I perked up and began to sing. I made sure Mary was getting dressed. She picked out a white blouse and her favorite pink pants. I couldn't wear pants to school, so I wore the blue and white pleated skirt and white blouse with puffy sleeves that Mama had sewed for me.

"Maggie, hurry up," Mike yelled. "It's your turn to watch for the bus."

I removed the night rag from my braids. Then I went to the front porch to watch for the bus.

The bus would always pass our house and pick up the kids who lived by the lake first. Half an hour later, it came back to pick up by brothers, me, Lewis (Aunt Louise and Uncle Ted's foster child), and the Harris kids.

"The bus just passed our house and is going toward the lake," I yelled.

After taking the twins to Mrs. Ollie, Mike dashed through the back door. "Is everyone ready for school?"

Thomas ran out of the bathroom, brushing his hair. Edward made sure he had his lunch.

"Here comes the bus up Wisner Road," I yelled from the front porch. "You have only a few minutes."

I rushed to the road. If anyone wasn't at the bus stop when the last person in line got on, you would get left behind. If that happened to anyone in our family, the choices were to find a ride to school or walk. If we were late, the Principal called Mama at the end of the day.

The Harris kids pushed and shoved, wanting to be first on the bus. I laughed, guessing that Jason Harris would be first. I looked to see if Mike was on his way. The bus came to a stop. I was the last in line and took baby steps, stalling for Mike. Finally, he dashed to the bus before the driver closed the door.

"That was a close one," I told him.

"I would've had to walk to school. Uncle Ted and Uncle John are already at work, and I sure wouldn't ask Aunt Louise to take me to school."

There were assigned bus seats. Once again, the colored kids had to sit in the back.

Mama had gone to the school many times and asked why our seats couldn't be moved closer to the front and if we could be picked up first. The school district said that it seemed easier to pick up the kids who lived around the lake first.

Last year there was one change. The school district let coloreds sit throughout the bus, but we still had to sit in the inside seats.

There were two more stops before our bus driver would turn into the residential area of White Cloud, follow the snake-like street, and stop at the elementary school.

The playground was crowded with kids. They chased each other or played on the swings, teeter-totters, or running to be the first to go down the slide.

I waited for Gloria, who shared a seat with me. She loved to talk with her friend, who sat across the aisle.

"Could you please walk a little faster?" I asked Gloria.

She looked back at me with a sharp eye. "I'm moving as fast as I can." She walked slower.

I saw Cheryl and Jackie outside. I knocked on the window and waved at them. I was surprised Sarah wasn't waiting for me with them. When I stepped off the bus, Sarah's bus pulled up. The four of us hurried into the wooded area next to the playground, where we'd make houses, something a lot of the girls did. We made ours in an area where the trees separated so we could have connected rooms.

"Hurry up! We don't want to lose our spot." I ran toward the trees, huffing and puffing.

Susan, a white girl I didn't get along with, came from across the playground, trying to beat me.

I ran faster. Cheryl, Jackie, and Sarah caught up with me, out of breath.

"Susan's group will have to go to another spot. Like over there." I pointed. "Those trees look good."

Susan despised colored people and had given me nothing but heartache since kindergarten. When I saw the frown on her face, I smiled.

My friends and I grabbed small tree branches and decided on a front door entrance. Cheryl made the living room while Jackie and Sarah made the bedrooms.

"Who's gonna make the bathroom?" Sarah asked. "It most certainly won't be me."

"It's not a real bathroom, so what difference does it make who builds it?" Jackie asked.

"Okay, Jackie. Since it doesn't matter, you can make it," Sarah said.

"I can't believe you're arguing over a make-believe

bathroom," I said. "Geez. Let's all make a wall. I'll make the window."

"Help!" I heard.

Teachers and kids were running toward the swings.

"I betcha some boy has either decided he's Superman, flying out of the swings, or someone fell off the teeter-totter," Jackie said.

"Probably Billy," I said. "He's always showing off."

By the time we reached the playground, the crowd had grown larger. Someone hollered, "It hurts!"

We jumped up and down, but couldn't see who it was.

"Is it Billy Atkins?" I asked a kid who could see more than us.

"No. Billy is standing over there." The kid pointed.

The school bell rang. The teachers and principal told everyone to leave the playground and walk to their class lines.

"Please stay in the line until your teacher arrives," the principal said.

There were lines for the early morning kindergarteners and for the first through fifth graders. The fifth grade girls stood together, and the boys did the same. Raymond bounced a basketball, playing Keep Away.

It took the principal a few minutes to get everyone's attention. "Everyone in fifth grade, please follow your teachers, Miss Carol and Mr. James. They will take you to the area where you will line up every morning for class."

The younger kids watched while we followed Miss Carol and Mr. James around the school.

When our class got to the other side, there wasn't any playground equipment, only two basketball courts. There were lots of trees next to an open area. Cheryl and I were in Miss Carol's class. Jackie and Sarah were in Mr. James' class.

"Everyone in my class, please get in line," Miss Carol

said. "The second bell will ring soon and then we'll go into the school."

I was second in line. Cheryl stood behind me. Mr. James' class lined up. I looked for Raymond.

"Class, we can go in," Miss Carol said.

The line began to move.

"Miss Dorsey, the line is waiting on you."

I tripped over my own feet and heard laughter from the kids.

"Are you all right?" Miss Carol asked.

With a soft voice, I said, "Yes." I walked slowly, pretending I wasn't embarrassed.

I still wanted to see if Raymond was in our line. I turned around. He ran to the back of the line for Mr. James' class. "Darn it," I said.

"Maggie," Cheryl said. "I didn't know you liked Raymond."

"What makes you think that?" I asked.

Cheryl just smiled and followed me into our room.

The boys shoved each other and picked the desks in the back.

"Boys, I'm happy to see your enthusiasm," Miss Carol said, "but I have assigned all of the seats."

The boys grumbled.

Miss Carol said, "I'll stand next to each desk and call a name. That will be your assigned desk for the year."

Cheryl's desk was two rows over from mine. I was assigned the third desk in the row next to the window. Susan's desk was in the row next to the door.

Miss Carol tapped her desk to get our attention. "Inside your desk, you'll find your class books. Please do not damage or lose them."

Everyone opened their desks. Some seemed excited to

be the first to use the books while others didn't seem too care. I was happy. I'd be the first to flip a page, and there were no torn, written-on, or missing pages.

"If the books are damaged," Miss Carol added, "your family will have to pay for them."

* * *

The next morning, instead of running to the east side of the playground with the little kids, Cheryl, Jackie, Sarah, and I ran to the west side, looking for a good place in the woods to make our house. We found a group of trees on a small hill that overlooked the high school.

"The next step to becoming a teenager," I told my friends.

"This is perfect," Sarah said.

"You're right," I said. "We can make our kitchen right here with a window that faces the high school. And..."

"And what?" Cheryl said.

"Susan," I mumbled.

My friends and I decided to ignore her. We turned our backs and continued to brush the leaves with branches to make the living room, bathroom, dining room, and bedrooms. She and her friends kicked the leaves in our house and walked further into the trees.

The first bell rang.

Once you had "tagged" your area by being the first one there, it was your space for the entire year and up to you to protect it.

My friends and I walked to get in our class lines. I turned around and saw Susan stop at our house. Her foot was in the air.

"Don't you dare!" I hollered.

Chapter 19

"Jackie, Cheryl, Sarah, Maggie and Susan. Today would be a good time to line up with the rest of the class," Miss Carol hollered.

I turned towards Miss Carol and then back to Susan. I squinted my eyes, hands on hip. "I mean it!" I said to Susan.

"And so do I," Miss Carol yelled back. "Get in line."

Susan swung her foot into our leaves. The class began to walk inside the building. Cheryl, Jackie and Sarah were at the end of the line. "Come on Maggie!" Cheryl hollered.

Susan and her friends caught the school door before it shut.

* * *

Our class had been in the fifth grade for four weeks. There were two rooms across the hall from ours designated for the sixth grade, but for now were empty.

After lunch the class ran to go outside, but were stopped

by Miss Carol and Mr. James. It was raining.

"Shoot," I said.

Miss Carol announced. "Okay everyone, please settle down. If the gym is open we can go there. If not, the boys can go to one of the empty rooms across the hall from our classrooms. Girls can go to the other."

While Mr. James, the other fifth grade teacher, went to see if the gym was available we lingered in the hallway by our classrooms.

This gave me and my friends a chance to peek around the corner at the younger kids.

"Don't you guys miss them?" I asked.

"In a way," Cheryl said shrugging her shoulders.

"Not me." Jackie frowned. "I don't miss none of those brats."

"Not even your cousin?" I pointed.

"I already see him too much."

Mr. James came back to our hallway. "There is a gym class inside. And, since no one can go outside, we'll have to hang out in the spare rooms across from our class."

Everyone moaned.

"Now, boys follow me."

Cheryl, Sarah, and Jackie were near the rest of our class, but I lingered behind to see if the rain had damaged our house outside under the trees when someone tapped my shoulder.

"What, are you looking at?" Miss Carol asked.

"Oh, nothing."

"Do you want to join the others in the room?"

"What was Miss Carol talking to you about?" Cheryl asked.

"Just to stay with the class."

"You checked on the house didn't you?" Sarah asked.

"Yeah. But, we're gonna have to wait until the last recess," I said.

"The leaves are probably soaking wet," Cheryl said.

"You guy and these houses," Jackie frowned. "I get enough of housekeeping at home."

When the bell rang for the last recess, the rain had stopped. The sun was shining. Sarah, Cheryl and myself impatiently ran to see our house. Jackie took her time.

The house was flattened with a water puddle in the middle of our living room. I looked over to where Susan had made her house. By the way she stomped her foot, it must had been in bad shape, too.

I brushed the leaves away that covered our secret spot where we placed the broach. "Thank God," I said. "It's still here. At least Susan didn't kick that up in the air."

Cheryl crossed her arms. "Look over there at Susan. She's standing while the other girls are trying to fix the house. She always acts like she's better than anyone."

"I know," Sarah said.

"My father told me that they didn't like coloreds," Jackie said. "He said for me to stay away from her."

"Sometimes, when she walks pass me I wanna trip her," I said.

"Come on Maggie," Cheryl said. "You know your mama has always told you that kindness hurts more."

Cheryl was right. Mama taught my brothers, sister and me to be good Christians. But I must admit that was hard to do. Susan's family enjoyed their summer home around the lake while our family worked the fields.

"Let's walk near the hill and see if there's a better place to make our house, further away from Susan," I said.

With the back of the high school in view, I pointed and told my friends that my brother Edward is down there in the seventh grade and Mike the eighth.

"Yep, and one more year, that's where we'll be," Jackie said. "I can't wait."

The school bell rang when Cheryl said, "We'll be there soon enough. But for now we have another year in the fifth and sixth grade right here."

The four of us wrapped our arms around each other's shoulders and walked in unison. Miss Carol and Mr. James yelled for the kids further in the woods to hurry before Principal Roberts check the halls.

* * *

The fifth grade was a growing up time for me. The classes seemed harder and the kids complained about the homework. Miss Carol would always say, "The classes are designed to prepare you all for the junior high."

I began to talk to Mama about racism and Susan, how every time I saw her I disliked her more. She reminded me of my faith and had me sit with our pastor for an hour after church service.

The first of the talks began when Pastor Johnson took off his robe and sat behind his office desk. "Maggie," he'd say clearing his throat, "your mother tells me that you have questions when it comes to your faith and keeping a kind heart."

I took a deep breath. "Pastor Johnson, there's this girl in my class. Her name is Susan."

Pastor Johnson interrupted. "You don't have to tell me her name. The name doesn't necessarily matter. Please continue."

"She calls me a name and snickers when she pass by me and my friends."

"What name is that?"

"Well..."

"You can tell me."

I played with my hands and shyly said, "Nigger."

"And how does that make you feel?"

"Mad. I'd walk up to her and point my finger in her face. I'd ask her what did you just say."

"What would she say back to you?"

"She always made it seem like it wasn't her. That I must had heard someone else."

Pastor Johnson walked from behind his desk and sat next to me. "Some people call coloreds that name because it is learned from one generation to the next. But, you shouldn't let their ignorance be replaced by your anger. I've been called all sorts of names and yes, it's hard to walk away, but I had to learn to have a thick skin. You're mother has told you about what having a thick skin is hasn't she?"

"Yes. It means you are bigger than you think and being able to walk away."

"Well, your mother had already told me some of what has been going on with you and a girl at your school. I gave her a scripture for the two of you to read together. But, I want you to read it by yourself as well. Okay?"

"Yes pastor."

"That's why I stopped you from telling me her name. Ignorance doesn't always have a name because by telling me her name won't stop her. Prayer and reading your scripture will. Do you understand?"

"Yes pastor."

"This Sunday, I'm going to preach a sermon on tolerance and if you like, we can meet after service to see how your week went and if the same desires to fight this girl was strong in my heart."

I had one hand on the door knob when Pastor Johnson asked if he could talk to me about another concern.

"Your mother told me that she . . . overheard a phone conversation between you and one of your friends. You were talking about a certain boy. I could have the First Lady speak to you."

"Pastor, I'm not kissing anyone," I stuttered. My friend has a boy she thinks that she likes and we were talking about that," I said.

Pastor Johnson gave me that pastoral smile. The soft one that reminded you of your religious commitment.

After I left his office I thought to myself, it wasn't a complete lie, so I won't die and go straight to hell will I?

It was lunch time in school the next day. While eating my potted meat sandwich I let my friends know that I had a meeting with Pastor Johnson, the pastor of our church, about Susan calling me a nigger.

"You told your pastor?" Sarah asked.

Cheryl interrupted. "What did he say?"

"He reminded me that I was a Christian and not to react in a negative way, meaning don't fight."

"Will you be able to do that. . .not fight?" Sarah asked.

"I'll have to or Mama will be called to the school."

Cheryl put her arms around me. "The three of us will make sure you don't hit her. Right Jackie?"

"Okay. I'll hold you back," Jackie reluctantly agreed. Sarah nodded.

"That wasn't the worst," I said. "He asked me about boys."

"What!" Cheryl said. "You told him about Raymond?"

"I lied, to my pastor! I told him that it was one of my other friends who had a boyfriend."

"Did he believe you?" Jackie asked.

"I don't know," I said. "He gave me one of those pastor-like smiles and told me that the First Lady could talk to me."

Ding. Ding.

"That's the bell," I said. "Please be careful when talkin' over the phone about boys. You know we have a three-way line and anyone can listen in."

* * *

It was near the end of the school year. All the students talked about was the sixth grade and anxious to initiate the incoming fifth grade class.

We ate inside because of the rain. Out of the corner of my eye I saw Susan.

"Can you believe that it's near the end of the school year, Maggie?" Cheryl asked.

I kept looking at Susan.

"You don't want to mess up now," Sarah said.

Susan walked by and said her usual comment. "Nigger." It flowed out of her mouth as if it was a part of speech.

Cheryl sat next to me. Underneath the table I squeezed her hand.

"Don't do it," Sarah told me.

Cheryl, Jackie, Sarah and I finished our lunch and kicked a ball around. There wasn't much room, so we kicked it softly. Accidentally, the ball went inside Susan and her friends' corner of the room.

"I'll go get it," Jackie said.

No matter how much we encouraged her to leave it, Jackie tried to walk over to their corner, but we held her back.

"Just like Maggie, I'm tired of that girl calling us names

and walking around like she's the queen of White Cloud."

"Jackie," I said. "Remember, how we're going help each other?" I reminded her.

Jackie kept saying but and stopped. She stood there staring at Susan. With our encouragement, she turned around and let the ball stay there.

The bell rung. Miss Carol came into the gym. "Hurry up girls. Time to get back to class."

Cheryl and I sat down whispering back and forth. Miss Carol taped on her desk.

"I'm placing your Geography tests on your desk. Each section is timed. When I say, please turn your test papers over and be ready to test on each of the four sections. Begin now."

The class had taken the last section of the test and turned them into Miss Carol.

She began to walk around the room. "In my hands the principal has instructed that I hand out this envelope to all of you and intended for your parents to read."

When she handed me my envelope I turned around and looked at my friend, Cheryl.

Cheryl raised her shoulders, a gesture that she didn't know what was inside and hadn't heard any gossip.

After she had passed out all of the envelopes, Miss Carol walked back to the front of the room and stood behind her desk.

She took a deep breath. "In another month-and-a-half, school will be out for the summer. The letter that I have just handed out will inform your parents that you will be attending the sixth grade — but at the high school building down the hill."

There was a silence-filled the room. Students looking at each other. Mouths held open. Then bursts of words from us. In one letter to our parents, everything was about to change.

www.ingramcontent.com/pod-product-compliance
Lightning Source LLC
Chambersburg PA
CBHW031418290426
44110CB00011B/427